# ANCIENT CULTURES

A Note About the Spelling of Names and Places in this Volume:

In the 1950s the Chinese introduced a romanization system called *pinyin*, designed to reproduce sounds more exactly, a system we have utilized in this volume. These spellings often differ markedly from the way we are accustomed to seeing them, however. To avoid confusion we have followed the *pinyin* spelling with the more familiar spelling following in parentheses. For instance: Kong Fuzi (Confucius), Laozi (lao-tse, Daode Jing (Tao-te-ching).

Published in 1996 by
Marshall Cavendish Corporation
99 White Plains Road
Tarrytown, NY 10591-9001
U.S.A.

*Editor*: Henk Dijkstra
*Executive Editor*: Paulien Retèl
*Revision Editors*: Rob van den Berg (Indo-Europeans in India, Cultures of the Pacific, Africa),
Frits Naerebout (The Early History of China)
Henk Singor (The Phoenicians, The Influence of the Phoenicians, The Israelites and Neighboring Peoples, Kings and Prophets, The Hittites, The Persians, Zarathushtra)
*Art Director*: Henk Oostenrijk, Studio 87, Utrecht, The Netherlands
*Index Editors*: Schuurmans & Jonkers, Leiden, The Netherlands
*Preface*: Suzanne Heim, Ph.D., Ancient Near East and Classical Art and Archaeology

*The History of the Ancient and Medieval World* is a completely revised and updated edition of *The Adventure of Mankind*.
©1996 by HD Communication Consultants BV, Hilversum, The Netherlands
This edition © 1996 by Marshall Cavendish Corporation, Tarrytown,
New York and HD Communication Consultants BV, Hilversum, The Netherlands

Library of Congress Cataloging-in-Publication Data

History of the ancient and medieval world / edited by Henk Dijkstra.
p. cm.
Completely rev. and updated ed. of :The Adventure of mankind (second edition 1996).
Contents:—v.3. Ancient Cultures.
ISBN 0-7614-0354-X (v.3).—ISBN 0-7614-0351-5 (lib.bdg.:set)
1. History, Ancient—Juvenile literature. 2. Middle Ages—History—Juvenile literature. I. Dijkstra, Henk. II. Title: Adventure of mankind
D117.H57 1996
930—dc20/95-35715

# History of the
# Ancient & Medieval World

## Volume 3

# Ancient
# Cultures

*Marshall Cavendish*
*New York   Toronto   Sydney*

# Ancient Cultures

Persian cylinder seal depicting Darius I during a hunting party

# CONTENTS

# Preface

The eastern and southern regions of the ancient world are as diverse as they are complex and distant, and yet they have been influenced by each other throughout history.

Ancient Near Eastern cultures of the second and the first millennum BC include states known for their political power, such as the Hittites of Anatolia in the second millennium. Their empire extended into Syria and were significant rivals of New Kingdom Egypt. Smaller kingdoms emphasizing international sea trade were established along the eastern Mediterranean coast by the Philistines in Canaan, the biblical enemy of the Israelites.

The Phoenicians to the north were also maritime explorers who established colonies in the western Mediterranean of the first millennium.

Among the most important of the empires to expand in the first millennium was that of the Achaemenid Persians based in southwestern Iran in the fifth and fourth centuries BC. Their control ranged to Anatolia and Egypt, only to be halted by Alexander the Great's conquest. The history of the Persians is bound up with that of the Indo-Europeans in Central Asia, to whom they are linguistically related. Migrations of the Indo-European peoples included Persians moving into Iran and Aryans into India, birthplace of the caste system and the Hindu religion. Both the ancient Persians and Greeks conquered parts of this region, allowing political and cultural interchange.

The ancient Israelites of the Old Testament lived in the biblical world of international power politics and struggles–from the age of the patriarch Abraham, to Moses of the Ten Commandments, to the united and divided kingdoms of Israel and Judah and the exile to Babylon.

Farther east, in China, the development of agriculture (c.7000 BC) and urbanization (c.1600 BC) began later than in the ancient Near East. A succession of dynasties ruled in different parts of a vast terrain that was organized into feudal states, where prominent philosophers, including Confucius, would come to have long-term worldwide influence.

To the south, in the Pacific Ocean, large island masses are home to a diverse group of cultures that arrived in a series of migrations beginning in 25,000 BC. Often differing racially and linguistically, they sometimes share cultural traits as well. Studies of the islands', modern native peoples have often led to conclusions about the lives of their early ancestors.

The rich continent of Africa, with its varied geography and climates, is where evidence of earliest man—homo sapiens—was found, dating to around 200,000 years ago. By 10,000 BC, three thousand ethnic groups had evolved, including four large language families with their multiplicity of cultures and geographical locations. Many other cultures connected profitably with the ancient Mediterranean, including the great Egyptian civilization that sprung up in the Nile Valley and the adventurous sea-faring Phoenicians.

*Suzanne Heim, Ph.D., Ancient Near East and Classical Art and Archaeology*

Phoenician statue of a woman wearing a variety of jewelry. It was made on Cyprus in the first half of the fourth century BC.

# The Phoenicians

## *Merchants of the Mediterranean*

There was a time when all of the known world was gathered around the Mediterranean Sea from the Middle Eastern coast to the Strait of Gibraltar. In this area could be found three great civilizations: Egypt, Crete, and Phoenicia. Hardy seamen and crafty traders, the Phoenicians became the carriers of the eastern world, the link between nations, gaining an almost complete monopoly on international commerce. On the Asian continent they concluded treaties with neighboring states that brought caravans bearing merchandise to Phoenician ports. Their maritime policy was even more striking. The

Reconstruction of a bronze cart that was made as a gift to the gods. The original of this cart was found during the excavations of Ugarit and was made in the second millennium BC.

Bronze statuette of a god found at the excavations of Ugarit, dating to the second millennium BC

shores of the Mediterranean were dotted with trading posts and warehouses crammed with local products carried by the fleets of Phoenicia to the East. About 260 miles (418 kilometers) northeast of Egypt, in an area that roughly approximates the coastal area of today's Lebanon and Syria, lay the strip of fertile coast occupied by the Phoenicians, bordered by the Lebanon Mountains to the east and the Mediterranean on the west. Phoenicia was about 200 miles (321 kilometers) long and 30 miles (48 kilometers) wide, and its people were distinguished for their long-distance commerce.

By 2000 BC the Phoenicians were an impressive and productive people with a civilization that was very different from their Egyptian neighbors. Like the Egyptians, the Phoenicians imported ivory, gold, and other raw materials that were used to make goods for export. But unlike the Egyptians, the Phoenicians were wholesalers, retailers, and transporters.

Tyre, which means "rock," was a characteristic Phoenician port, the greatest Phoenician city-state. It had two harbors and a town closely packed with houses, some of them several stories, built on the rocks. It was an island fortress, established partly on the mainland, but largely on an offshore island, and within it dwelled a growing population of timber merchants, shipbuilders, sailors, weavers, and cloth dyers. Phoenicia was the land of the famed Cedars of Lebanon, a treasure to the Egyptians, whose own land held almost nothing but palm trees, and who had been building their boats from

papyrus reeds. In fact, the earliest recorded sea voyage, 800 miles (1287 kilometers) and back, took place around 2600 BC, when the Egyptians sailed to the Phoenician port of Byblos to buy forty shiploads of cedar. The sea was everything to the Phoenicians; even its shore's white sand was the source of the transparent glass they profitably exported.

It was natural that the Phoenicians turned to the sea for their livelihood, and it was their experience in carrying their exports across the sea that gained them the reputation of the world's first explorers. Their land was ideally situated for trade, halfway between two prosperous nations: Egypt and the land of the Hittites, on the main caravan routes between northern Africa and the Mesopotamian countries.

They didn't conduct trade exclusively by sea, carrying goods overland as far as Babylon, but the Phoenicians were best known as seafaring traders and merchants who founded small colonies all over the Mediterranean, gaining wealth for their cities. Phoenicia even established a trading post in the heart of commercial Egypt, at Memphis. They were the chief sailors on the Mediterranean for many centuries in the early first millennium BC because of their sailing vessels and their seamanship. The Phoenician ships had a flat keel and a curved stem. A double deck offered space for two rows of oarsmen. With these light ships they crossed the Mediterranean and even dared to go to the Atlantic and Indian Oceans. The Phoenician captains made observations on shores, distances, landmarks, currents, and

wind direction. They possessed a wealth of precise navigational knowledge. People in other countries in need of ships or sailors got them from the Phoenician city-states.

Israel's King Solomon entered into a trade agreement with Phoenician King Hiram of Tyre (in 950 BC) to do business with the people living on the coast of the Red Sea. The arrangement probably extended to inhabitants of western Arabia or beyond, the

land of Ophir in the Bible. The pharaohs of Egypt hired Phoenicians to help them build and sail their own fleets and equip their expeditions. Later, in the fifth and fourth centuries BC, both Persian kings and Alexander the Great would put the vast sea-faring experience of the Phoenicians to use.

The country where the Phoenicians lived offered little opportunity to make a living by any means other than trade and navigation, living as they did on a narrow strip of land along the east coast of the Mediterranean, backed by two mountain chains, the Lebanon and the Anti-Lebanon. The high mountains came so close to the sea that there was little room left for farmland or cities. In ancient times, both mountain chains were

The remains of a royal tomb, dating from the second millennium BC. It was found near the ancient city of Byblos.

Bronze statue of a Phoenician goddess from the first millennium BC

297

Phoenician
necklace with gold
pendants
(seventh century BC),
excavated in Spain

Small statue depicting
a woman. It was made in the
first millennium BC,
and found in the ruins of
Sidon.

covered with the extensive cedar and cypress forests that provided the rot-resistant wood especially useful in the shipbuilding industry. According to ancient historic records, the pharaohs used this Phoenician wood for both their private boats and their holy ships. King Solomon imported cedar from Lebanon for use as the beams of his temple in Jerusalem (950 BC). Despite its dearth of fertile land, Phoenicia had essential export commodities in its lumber and famous woven textiles dyed purple, a color derived from the creamy colored liquid of the shellfish called *Murex* or *Purpura* that abounded in the Mediterranean. It was such dyed cloth that became the standard for royal purple. The word *Phoenician* comes from a Greek word, phoenix, meaning "red-purple."

The earliest information about the Phoenicians is recorded in Phoenician inscriptions dating as early as the thirteenth and twelfth centuries BC from the coast of the present-day Lebanon (for example, at Byblos) and from Cyprus. Otherwise, much of our knowledge about them comes from the later Greek texts of Homer (eighth century BC), the Roman historian Pliny (first century AD), and Philo of Byblos (second century AD).

As a people, the Phoenicians may have been rooted in the Canaanite culture of the eastern coast of the Mediterranean Sea in the second millennium BC. In the book of Genesis in the Bible, Phoenicia is in fact called the eldest son of Canaan. The Phoenician language, similar to the Canaanite, was one of the many Semitic languages long in use in the ancient Near East.

Another important center of international trade was Ugarit near the coast in northern Syria (1550–1200 BC). Its artifacts and architecture have similarities to those found at Phoenician sites farther south like Byblos, Sidon, and Tyre. The Phoenician centers took over the trade in Cypriot copper, the essential ore for bronze-working, from Ugarit after its destruction around 1200 BC.

## Independent Kingdoms

Protected by the mountains at their backs and lacking any need for central organization against a threat of foreign invasion, the Phoenician centers remained politically separate. This structure led to the creation of a loose federation composed of independent kingdoms or city-states. The Phoenicians never formed a unified empire.

The city of Byblos was a major trading partner with Egypt, but was soon overshadowed by Sidon. This city became so powerful that both Homer and the Bible referred to the Phoenicians as Sidonians. Phoenician carpenters and construction workers were recruited for Solomon's temple construction in Jerusalem, because, according to the Bible, nobody could work with wood as well as the Sidonians. In fact, the Phoenician laborers who worked in Jerusalem did not actually come from Sidon, but from Tyre. In the days of the Homeric epics (about the eighth century BC), ancient Sidon had already been overshadowed by Tyre for some time. Today, Sidon is just a modest fishing village, covering a small area of the old city. In the past it was famous for its gardens, and its suburbs extended well into the plains.

Tyre was located on a small island about a mile (1.6 kilometers) off the coast. Owing to the lack of space, its houses were several stories high—according to Strabo, the Roman geographer of the first century BC—many with more floors than the houses in Rome. Some of the city's drinking water had to be imported from the mainland, which left Tyre vulnerable in case of siege. The city had two harbors, the Sidonian (which has gradually filled with silt) on the north side of the island and the Egyptian, still in existence today on the south side. A considerable part of the island was taken up by the temple of the god Melkart-Baal-Tsor (meaning the Lord of Tyre). This temple contained not only conse-

Ruins of the ancient city of Ugarit (1400–1200 BC). Here, the famous archive of tablets written in an early alphabetic cuneiform script was found during excavation campaigns.

crated rooms but housed buildings for the civil government. Melkart is sometimes identified with the Greek god Hercules. In the Bible, he is referred to as Moloch. Melkart was the god of navigation and trade. The colonies of Tyre sent him gifts every year and Tyre sailors came home for the annual Melkart feasts.

## Politics and Trade Interests

A king and a council of elders governed each of the Phoenician cities. These elders

This little terra-cotta statue represents a pregnant woman, sitting on a backless chair.
In the fifth century BC, when it was made, people thought that having such a statuette would make childbirth easier. It was found in a Phoenician cemetery in Akhziv, south of Tyre.

appointed magistrates entrusted with the administration of daily government. On occasion an important family would succeed in garnering control of all positions. (This would happen later in the trade republic of Venice.) At times they succeeded in establishing virtual dynasties, making the highest posts hereditary. More often, though, these dynasties were routed out through the joint efforts of other prominent families, only to see another dynasty rise in its stead. This was a frequent pattern in Carthage, a colony of Tyre.

One of the Tyre dynasties was closely tied to King Solomon. Three generations of this family governed Tyre, beginning with King Aben-Baal (son of Baal) and his son Hiram.

The stone sarcophagus of Eshmunazar II, king of Sidon in the sixth century BC. It was found when ancient Sidon was excavated.

The grandson of Hiram was assassinated and replaced by a priest of Astarte. (Merchants may have installed the priest on the throne intentionally to prevent further dynastic disputes. The priest may also have been the puppet of a powerful family desirous of power but unwilling to accept the risk of direct rule.) Similar dynasties governed in Sidon.

The merchants of Tyre and Sidon could rightfully claim that their empire was located on the ocean waves rather than on the little island. Many families owned property overseas; some ruled entire islands. They would frequently return home, having made a fortune abroad, bringing a sense of the exotic in their clothing and new habits. The biblical prophet Ezekiel pointed out the cosmopolitan nature of Tyre. He listed the regions with which the Phoenicians did business as from Asia Minor to Egypt and from Arabia to the south of Spain. Such far-reaching business contacts required the merchants to have extensive knowledge of the merchandise available in the various countries where they traded. They had to have good ships and an understanding of navigation.

## Carthage and Other Phoenician Colonies

At a great many strategic points along the Mediterranean coastline, the Phoenicians owned warehouses and trading posts. Over the years, some of these developed into large colonies and cities. Carthage in present-day Tunisia is the most famous. The city was founded in 800 BC by a group of discontented or exiled citizens of Tyre, forced to leave their country for political reasons. They landed near Utica, an older colony of Tyre. They founded a new colony they called Qart-hadasht (new city). The Greeks called it Carchédon; the Romans, Carthago. The city was located on a bay and enjoyed a natural harbor, among the best harbors of the Mediterranean.

The Phoenicians had a knack for finding such strategic places. They founded Marseilles before the Greeks settled there. Barcelona, Málaga, Algeciras, and Cádiz (in Spain) were also Phoenician settlements. Cádiz was the last stop before crossing the Atlantic, en route to what were called the tin islands. These were Great Britain and Brittany, essential sources of the tin needed to meld with copper to form the alloy bronze. The indigenous people there exchanged hides and tin for fabric and other goods they could not make. Especially popular were the purple textiles made only by the Phoenicians.

The Phoenicians never organized a colonial empire. Only trade relationships and a vague sense of kinship existed between the colonies and the mother towns. That was sufficient, however, to cause the Phoenician cities to refuse to wage war against Carthage when the Persian King Cambyses tried to force them to do so in the sixth century (c.525 BC) to help in expanding his empire.

The ruins of the Phoenician city of Tyre, which once was the largest marketplace of the Mediterranean

# The Influence of the Phoenicians

*Exploratory Expeditions, Religion, and the Alphabet*

In the early centuries of the first millennium BC, if not before, the Phoenicians were noted as great and daring seafarers. They traveled from their bases in Syria and Palestine to previously unknown regions, whether on their own initiative or for the benefit of others.

**Exploratory Voyages to Africa**
The Phoenicians are thought to have sailed

301

around the African continent about 600 BC, commissioned by the Egyptian pharaoh Necho. The Greek historian Herodotus writes of this expedition in the fifth century BC:

"They sailed south along the coast. In winter, the fleet looked for a safe haven where they sowed grain. After the harvest, the Phoenician ships moved on with fresh provisions on board. This way, the voyage around Africa took three years. The ships departed from the Red Sea and returned to the Mediterranean via the Strait of Gibraltar."

After their return home, the Phoenician sailors claimed that they saw the sun to the north. While this was unbelievable to their contemporaries (and possibly to Herodotus, who reported it merely as an interesting anecdote), it lends credence to the story that the Phoenicians passed the equator. In the Northern Hemisphere, the midday sun appears slightly to the south because the earth is tilted on its axis. The reverse is true in the Southern Hemisphere: The sun appears to the north at midday. The Phoenician voyage around Africa may well have taken place. Their story is all the more plausible because of the two winters they were said to have spent on land. As a result of this voyage, the continent of Africa was found to be surrounded by the sea.

One of the most famous voyages was the Phoenicians' exploration of the African coast from the Mediterranean port of Carthage, situated on the northern shore of the continent. They sent a number of expeditions west through the Strait of Gibraltar and then southward along the western coast.

The Greek translation of a Phoenician shipping log from the late fifth century BC has survived, stored in customary fashion in the temple of the god Baal Hammon in Carthage. It reports:

Phoenician
bronze statue of a
goddess
that was made in the first
millennium BC

302

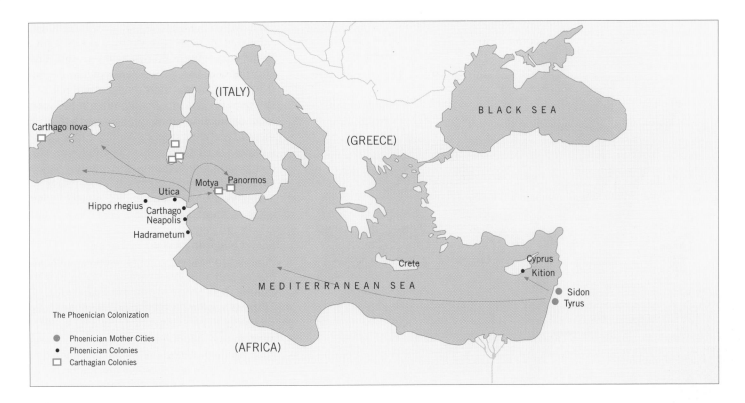

The Phoenician Colonization

● Phoenician Mother Cities
• Phoenician Colonies
□ Carthagian Colonies

"By the Senate of the city of Carthage, it was determined that Hanno would sail past the Pillars of Hercules to found colonies. He departed with sixty ships, each with fifty rowers. On board were men, women, and children, totaling thirty thousand. Two days after we had sailed past the Strait of Gibraltar, we founded a city we named Thymiaterion. From there to Cape Libya stretched a vast, tree-covered plain. There we built a temple for Poseidon, the god of the sea, and then sailed on to the south. We reached a lake where there were elephants and other wild animals. After another day of travel we founded new colonies and reached the river Lixos [probably the River Draa]. A tribe of Berber [Moroccan] shepherds lived on the banks of this river with their flocks; we befriended them and rested for a few days. Even further the inhospitable 'Ethiopians' lived in a mountainous land that was teeming with wild animals. After sailing on for three days, we arrived in a bay where the island of Cerne is located [the mouth of the Gold River]. There we founded a colony. We believe this place to be located as far to the west of the Pillars of Hercules as Carthage is to the east. We sailed a river [the Senegal] upstream until we reached a lake with islands. On the banks of this lake rose great mountains. On their slopes roamed wild people dressed in animal skins who pelted us with stones. From there we came to another wide river with many crocodiles and hippopotamuses. We then returned to Cerne and sailed southward for twelve days. All of this land was inhabited by 'Ethiopians' [or black Africans; Ethiopia is actually in northeast Africa] who disappeared as soon as we went ashore. Finally we reached mountains that were covered with many-colored trees bearing a pleasant aroma. For two days we

Small Roman statuette representing a ship with two Phoenician sailors.
The Phoenicians were known as very able merchants on the seas, but they also became notorious for piracy.

303

Phoenician statuette
of a man on horseback
carrying a round
shield

lake, within which another island was to be found. Many wild 'people' live there, mainly females. Their bodies were completely covered with hair, and our interpreters called them gorillas. We tried to catch one but we did not succeed in catching a male because they climbed into the trees and defended themselves with stones. We did catch three females, but because they bit everyone, we had to kill them. After we had skinned them, we took their hides to the city of Carthage."

Hanno seems to have sailed at least as far south as Sierra Leone.

## Secret Shipping Logs

Phoenician shipping logs were doubtless maintained with great care and considerable caution. It is assumed that the reason so few of them remain is that they were kept so secret that few copies or translations were ever made. Most trading nations closely guarded their sources of income to keep the fruits of their exploration to themselves. (The Portuguese of the sixteenth century, for instance, would not reveal the location of the

sailed along this mountainous coast and then arrived at a large lake that our interpreters called 'the Horn of the West.' We went ashore to replenish our supply of drinking water, but became fearful of the countless fires we saw all around us and of the noise of flutes, cymbals, and drums. Loud shouts sounded as well. We then sailed for four days along the coast of a country that was on fire; at night it seemed as if the flames reached the sky. We then reached a mountain that we named the 'Hill of the gods.' Three days later we arrived at a gulf called 'the Horn of the South.' In this gulf was an island with a

Phoenician stele from
the fourth century BC. It was
found during the
excavations of Amrit, which
is north of Byblos.

304

Stone stele from the fourth century BC, with a picture of a man sacrificing to the gods. It comes from Carthage.

Statue of the Egyptian pharaoh Osorkon I (tenth century BC) found during excavations in Byblos

Moluccas, a valuable source of herbs and spices.) The Phoenicians maintained their trade secrets in the Atlantic so thoroughly that neither the Greeks nor the Romans learned who their trading partners were.

There is an account of a Phoenician ship that deliberately changed course and ran aground when a Roman ship was observed to be spying on it. The Roman vessel, following its target, was also shipwrecked. Only the captain of the Phoenician ship survived. When he finally returned home from the Atlantic, he was rewarded for the clever way he tricked the Romans. His city honored him and gave him large sums of money,

including full compensation for his lost cargo. Through the strict confidentiality they maintained and the horrifying accounts they told of life at sea, the Phoenicians confined other nations to the Mediterranean Sea. They kept the Atlantic for themselves for centuries.

It is not clear if and when Phoenician navigational knowledge reached the Greeks, but books on navigation did exist. Greek sailors on the island of Rhodes compiled *The Captain of the Mediterranean*, a book that contained everything they knew about trade routes, winds, and ocean currents. It described the most favorable times for crossing the sea and proffered advice on avoiding bad

305

Bronze statuette of the Canaanite god Baal

The Phoenicians developed clever, self-serving methods for trading with indigenous people. According to Herodotus, the Carthaginians would sail to the west coast of Africa each year at an appointed time. They would deposit the goods they wanted to trade on the beach and return to their ships. The natives would then emerge from the jungle and place as much gold next to the merchandise as they saw fit. The Phoenicians would then return to determine whether the amount of gold was sufficient. If it was not, they would go back to their ships without touching anything. The natives would then add more gold. This game would sometimes be repeated several times before the parties came to an agreement. Only then would the Phoenicians accept the gold and embark, leaving the natives to take the goods.

Despite this story, the Phoenicians had a reputation for dishonesty with the Greeks. In Homer's epic, the *Odyssey*, the swineherd Eumaeus tells his life story to Odysseus, granting the Phoenicians a less than honorable role. According to the tale, Phoenician traders arrived at his father's house one day "with thousands of objects to sell; but they came as wolves with a false heart." They camped near the city for a year before kidnapping the boy Eumaeus and persuading his nurse to flee with them, taking all her master's gold and silver. Eumaeus recounts:

"On the day of departure, the servant took me to the ship with the stolen gold. As soon as we were on board, the ship set out to sea and the wind billowed the sails. For six days and six nights we sailed, and on the seventh day my wet nurse fell into the sea and was eaten by the fish. The wind and the waves took us to Ithaca, and here Laertes bought me, along with other goods."

This passage from the *Odyssey* gives an interesting glimpse into the trading practices of the Phoenicians. Presumably, they were

weather, rounding the ocean capes, and benefiting from the wind. Until the nineteenth century, it remained an indispensable manual for vessels navigating the Mediterranean.

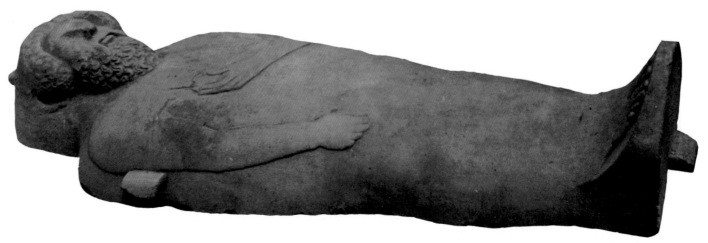

The lid of a Phoenician coffin. It was found in modern Cádiz in Spain, once a Phoenician colony called Gades.

Phoenician
mask

unhurried, allowing their customers to inspect their goods at leisure. They apparently sold only merchandise of good quality. This is corroborated by Phoenician artifacts, such as metal vessels, that have been excavated. All are finely crafted, made of good-quality raw materials. Evidently, however, if they could rob their customers as they departed, they would do so, even kidnapping to make more money. This practice was not exclusively Phoenician. Many ancient nations captured people to sell as slaves.

The Phoenicians were apparently both admired and feared by the Greeks. They were pirate merchants who offered the as-yet-undeveloped Greece luxury products from much-more-developed eastern civilizations.

## Mystery Cults

While Phoenician religion was derived from the Canaanite beliefs in the second millennium BC, each city had its own deities, some totally new and different. Much of our information comes from Greek and Roman sources, giving us the classical equivalents of the Near Eastern names.

Tammuz (the Greek Adonis) was the son of Baal (the god of rain and fertility) and Astarte (the goddess of fertility and love). The Romans formed a cult to worship

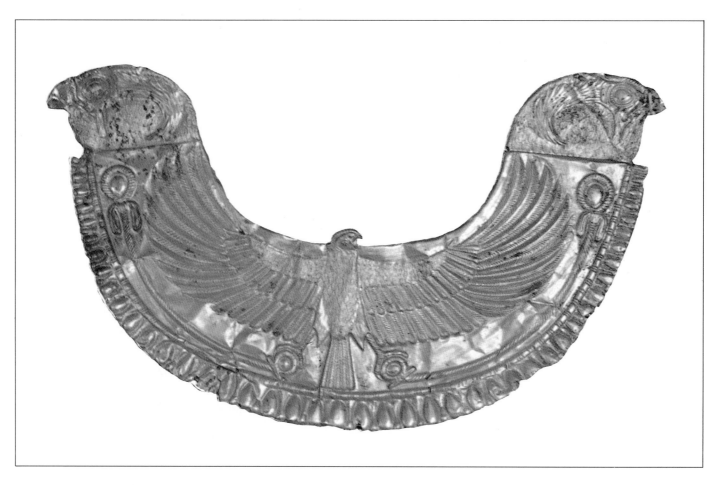

As a result of the trade contacts between the two countries, pre-Phoenician (Canaanite) art was influenced by Egypt. This gold breastplate, in Egyptian style, was found in a grave near Byblos.

Astarte, the mother-goddess, and Tammuz, her divine son. They were especially popular among the Romans, who showed great interest in eastern mysteries. Tammuz (Adonis) was the god of agriculture, symbolically dying with the crops each winter, to be reborn in the spring. Water sources became important as places to worship him. In arid and mountainous Phoenicia, the annual sprouting of new vegetation was nothing less than a miracle. All Phoenician colonies and settlements adopted the cult's winter and spring holidays. In the third century AD, they were still celebrated in many cities of the Roman Empire with offerings and festivals.

## The Alphabet

The most important legacy of the Phoenicians is undoubtedly the alphabet. The earliest forms of writing were pictographs meant to express ideas, like the Egyptian hieroglyphs, ancient Mayan picture writing, or the written symbols of today's Chinese and Japanese. When a pictograph or ideograph comes to represent the sound of the word rather than what is drawn or the idea behind it, an alphabet begins. The first known alphabet, called North Semitic, evidently originated on the eastern Mediterranean shore between 1700 and 1500 BC. It consisted only of consonants, as do today's

related Hebrew and Arabic alphabets. Other branches, including Phoenician and Hebrew variants, developed from the original Semitic alphabet in the eleventh century BC.

There are no traces of a Phoenician pictography. Phoenician inscriptions utilized an alphabet. In 1876, a Syrian farmer discovered copper beakers with inscriptions from the time of King Hiram of Tyre, about 950 BC. The man broke the beakers to sell the metal. Only a few fragments with inscriptions were recovered, which are now in the Louvre Museum in Paris. The writing system used on them is the known Semitic script. It reads from right to left and uses the peculiar linear signs of the alphabet.

The letters of the alphabet are probably simplifications of old Semitic pictographs. According to the Greeks, the alphabet was given to them by Kadmos (which means "the

Ivory carving with a goddess feeding two goats. She is probably a goddess of fertility, and for that reason one of the most important Near Eastern deities (thirteenth century BC). From a site near Ugarit

The city of Gebal (ancient Byblos). In the foreground are some pre-Phoenician temple ruins, on the left is the temple of the Obelisks, and in the background are the outskirts of the city as it is now.

man from the east"). Herodotus reports that the Greeks adopted the alphabet from the Phoenicians (living to their east) and made only minor changes to the shape of the letters. It is not surprising that the Greek word for book, *biblion*, derives from Byblos, the Phoenician city. The alphabet's Semitic origins are evident in the names of the letters. These have meaning in the Semitic languages but bear none in Greek. For example, *alpha*, represented by the letter *A*, has no meaning in Greek, whereas the Hebrew *aleph* means oxen. The letter *B*, *beta* in Greek, was derived from the Hebrew *beth*, meaning house. The Greek *gamma* or *G*, is a corruption of *gimel*, the Hebrew word for camel. *D* is *delta* in Greek and *daleth*, or door, in Hebrew, and so forth.

In 1922, a number of royal tombs were discovered in Byblos. The stone coffin of the early tenth-century BC king Ahiram contained an elaborate text in the linear Phoenician alphabet. An early Semitic text is the stele inscription of King Mesha of Moab in Transjordan, an enemy of the kings of Israel (ninth century BC). The campaigns mentioned in his inscription are also chronicled in the books of the Bible. This Canaanite sovereign used an alphabet related to the Phoenician and Hebrew for his victory text. This demonstrates that the Phoenician alphabet spread rather quickly in the Near

Terra-cotta mask of a Phoenician god from the sixth century BC, found in Cagliari.

310

Monument for
King Mesha of Moab
(ninth century BC), inscribed
in an alphabetic script
similar to Phoenician and
Hebrew. This script
formed the basis for the Greek
and Latin alphabets.

East.

The Phoenicians claimed, according to the Christian bishop Eusebius (c. AD 260–339) that they had not really invented the alphabet, but had simplified and improved an existing writing system. This seems to coincide with the Phoenician tendency to adaptation in the arts and religion from other nations. Regardless, the Phoenicians were responsible for the alphabet's spread.

The Phoenician settlements on the Mediterranean shore between Aradus and Acre were surrounded by four groups that each had a script. They were the Hittites to the north, the Cretans and Mycenaeans to the west, the Babylonians and the Assyrians to the east, and the Egyptians to the south.

The Hittites used hieroglyphs of such complexity that their script has still not been deciphered. The Cretans and the Mycenaeans had only a rudimentary pictography at their disposal (called Linear A and B) which they themselves had recently adopted. The Mesopotamians' cuneiform script used symbols for each syllable without attempting to simplify the script. In Egypt, in the second millennium BC, a script called the sacerdotal was developed, in addition to the hieroglyphs already in use. This script drew the hieroglyphs in an abbreviated form, much as modern stenography writes the alphabet in short form. The sacerdotal script bears some similarity to an alphabetical script, but contains as many symbols as the hieroglyphs. It constituted a change in writing method but not in structure. The sacerdotal script was disseminated to some extent in the lands around Egypt. Inscriptions of Semitic foremen working in the service of Egyptians have been found in the turquoise mines of the Sinai desert. The symbols used here were derived from the sacerdotal script and had been reduced to simple lines. It was a simple script suitable for jotting down short notes in the mines. It is possible that the Phoenicians were familiar with it.

Regardless of the alphabet's origin, the Phoenicians developed a new system of only twenty-two consonant symbols. In turn, the Greeks adopted the alphabet from the Phoenicians in the eighth century BC. They expanded the twenty-two Phoenician consonants to twenty-four and made some symbols serve as vowels. They wrote from left to right after about 500 BC. Their alphabet was adopted and adapted throughout the Mediterranean world, most importantly by the Romans. They then spread it via Latin by conquest to all of western Europe.

Moses climbs Mount Sinai; miniature from a Greek manuscript from the twelfth century AD

# The Israelites and Neighboring Peoples

## From Patriarch Abraham to the Lawgiver Moses

The region of ancient Israel and Palestine lies on the eastern shore of the Mediterranean Sea. Its fertile plains along the coast give way farther inland to the hills and mountains of Galilee, Samaria, and Judaea. The Jordan River, the only major water supply in the region, runs parallel to the Mediterranean shore for 100 miles (160 kilo-meters), separating it from Transjordan. It flows south to the Sea of Galilee and beyond, through one of the world's deepest canyons, to the saline waters of the Dead Sea, lying 1,310 feet (400 meters) below sea level, the lowest place on earth. (The Sea of Galilee, more than 650 feet [200 meters] below sea level, is the only large freshwater lake in the

313

Ruins of the ziggurat at Ur, the city in Mesopotamia where Abraham came from. Abraham left Ur with his family for the promised land of Canaan.

area.) The rocky plateau of Transjordan begins on the eastern bank of the river. From there the desert stretches all the way to Mesopotamia. The passes through Carmel and Lebanon in the north give access to Syria and the Euphrates Valley. South across the Negev Desert and the Sinai Peninsula lies Egypt.

Located where the natural routes to three continents meet, the coastal region has always been a place of intercultural contact

Philistine pot. The Philistines were one of the peoples who settled in the coastal area between Mount Carmel and Egypt in the late second millennium BC. Since that time the region has been called Philistina, or Palestina.

and conflict. Some of the earliest agricultural communities developed here during the Neolithic era, from about 9300 BC. Archaeological evidence indicates that a mixed population existed in the region even as early villages developed into city-states by the third millennium BC.

Neighboring Egypt, one of the predominant powers in the region, was always a threat and succeeded in establishing a hegemony in the area in the second millennium BC. This would be challenged unsuccessfully by invading Amorites, Hittites, and Hurrians.

During the third millennium BC, Semitic-speaking peoples lived alongside the Sumerians in Mesopotamia and eventually established a new ruling dynasty (the Akkadians). Other Semitic groups with powerful kingdoms of their own were in Syria, as at Ebla and Mari. At this time there were also movements of nomadic peoples throughout the ancient Near East who intruded upon the urban centers. These included the West Semitic Amorites ("Amurru") who made their way into southern Mesopotamia as well as into western Syria.

By the beginning of the second millennium, the area west of the Jordan River is culturally known as the greater land of Canaan. The culture of the Canaanites characterizes the area until the destruction of the major centers in the eastern Mediterranean around 1200 BC. The invading newcomers, known as the "Sea Peoples," included the Philistines who settled along the southern coast. The origin of the name *Palestine* comes from this group and was first used by the Greeks.

## Abraham, the Patriarch

The family of Abraham (originally named Abram) lived in the city of Ur, on the lower reaches of the Euphrates in southern Mesopotamia. Abraham is generally assumed to have lived between 2000 and 1800 BC. Because he is principally important as the founder of Judaism and the Jewish people as well—who are said to be descendants of Isaac, the son of his old age—Abraham plays the unusual dual role of the founder of not only a religion, but a race. His titles, Father of the Faithful and Friend of God, are used by Muslims who also look upon the man they call Ibraham as ancestor of the Arabs, through Ishmael. In yet another religion, Christianity, heaven is described as "the Bosom of Abraham," and the sacrifice of Isaac is often depicted as the epitome of faith among men.

Ur was one of Sumer's major city-states. The city is also known as Ur of the Chaldees, an important cultural and commercial center.

Among the remains are a royal cemetery and the Temple of Ninhursag at Ubaid, bearing the inscriptions of the kings of the first dynasty. The Akkadian period, after the capture of the city by Sargon in 2340, marks an important step in the blending of Sumerian and Semitic cultures. In 2060 King Ur-

Nammu built a gigantic ziggurat, or temple tower, dedicated to the moon-god Nanna. It has stood, although crumbled and covered with sand, throughout the centuries. Here also was discovered the oldest known law code yet discovered, the code of Ur-Nammu, which predates the code of Hammurabi by 300 years. The third dynasty of Ur fell to the Elamites and later to Babylon. Various kings and queens later destroyed and rebuilt Ur, including Nebuchadnezzar. In the plains

Terra-cotta model of an Aramaean house, used as an *ossuary* (container for bones of the deceased)

Seventeenth-century AD oil painting
of Abraham's sacrifice, as it is described in
the Book of Genesis in the Bible.
God tested Abraham's faith by asking
him to sacrifice his son Isaac with a knife,
but when Abraham was about to
kill his son, an angel blocked his hand. ❯

The valley of the
Orontes River in Syria,
the fertile region in the land
of the Amorites

Terra-cotta head,
probably portraying a god.
It was made around
500 BC.

316

around Ur, Semitic nomads put their herds
out to pasture and brought food to the city.
Some of them settled in Ur, usually maintaining ties with their relatives.

Abram married his half sister Sara and left
Ur, taking his father Terah and his nephew
Lot and Lot's family. Believing that God
would make him a "great nation," Abram
moved on toward Canaan, as God commanded. They took the traditional route that various nomadic groups must have taken, following the Euphrates upstream to Padan-
Aram (Harran) in Syria. Here, Abram's
father died, and he and Lot went south, making their first encampment at Shechem,
where Genesis adds: "And the Canaanites
were then in the land."

## The Land of the Canaanites

Evidently due to famine in Canaan, Abram
moved south to Egypt, where he was ousted
for claiming Sara as his sister. Back in
Canaan, Abram sought the support and aid
of his Canaanite kinsmen. The new arrivals
prospered, but eventually quarreled and separated. Abram gave Lot first choice of lands
and cattle. Lot chose the best pastures of the
valley of the Jordan, remaining near Sodom,
and Abram departed. He subsequently
returned to rescue Lot from the invading
King Chedorlaomer of Elam, for which he
was blessed by Melchizedek, king of Salem
(Jerusalem). God promised him a son by
Sara. In a covenant with God, Abram
promised to have himself and his people cir-
cumcised in exchange for the rights to
Palestine forever. After the covenant was
renewed, the rite of circumcision was established. Abram was henceforth called
Abraham and Sara was called Sarah. Sarah
delivered the baby Isaac when Abraham was
a hundred (biblical) years old. Isaac was his
first legitimate descendant. After Sarah died,
Abraham married Keturah and had another
six sons by her. According to Genesis, he
died at age 175. He is believed to be buried
with Sarah in the Cave of Machpelah (in
Hebron, on the West Bank).

Many of the customs described in the Old
Testament of the Bible show great resem-
blance to those of Mesopotamia and Syria.
The obvious similarities seem based on the

common customs of Semitic, Hurrian, and other peoples of the ancient Near East. Illustrations of this influence are the Sumerian stories of the Creation and the Flood, both biblical as well, and later numerous details of everyday life, including laws governing marriage and inheritance.

Abraham, who was originally childless with Sarah, adopted his servant Eliezer as an heir, a custom sanctioned in the Babylonian Code of Hammurabi (eighteenth century BC). Abraham's wife Sarah gave her husband a young Egyptian slave woman, Hagar; to bear him children who would also be Sarah's. This practice is recommended in the same code. Ishmael, first son of Abraham, was born when Abraham was eighty-six (biblical) years old. Because of Ishmael's mother, Hagar, Abraham (Ibrahim) is also regarded as a patriarch of the Arabs.

### Ties with Egypt

Isaac, son of Abraham and Sarah, and his wife Rebekah, according to the Old Testament, bore Jacob, the Hebrew patriarch and grandson of Abraham. Genesis details how Jacob tricked his twin brother Esau out of his birthright and fled to his uncle, Laban. Esau is later identified with the kingdom of Edom as Jacob is with Israel. Jacob married Laban's daughters, Leah and Rachel. They and their servants bore him the twelve sons who established the twelve tribes of Israel: Leah's sons Reuben, Simeon, Levi, Judah, Issachar, and Zebulun; Rachel's sons Joseph and Benjamin; servant Bilhah's sons Dan and Naphtali; and servant Zilpah's sons Gad and Asher. Jacob and some seventy members of his family subsequently left Canaan, possibly fleeing famine, for the fertile soil of the Nile Delta where their people would spend several centuries.

Biblical scholars interpret all this as tribal history. They agree that some of the tribes migrated to Egypt. This may have happened during the mid-seventeenth to mid-sixteenth centuries BC, when the Semitic Hyksos kings conquered Egypt. When the Hyksos were deposed, the Hebrews may have been persecuted and enslaved by the Egyptian rulers.

Near the Nile in Egypt is the site of

Egyptian *faience* (glazed quartz) face of Bes, a god of music

Isaac meets Rebekah, his future wife. They bore twin sons, Jacob and Esau. Jacob, in his turn, raised twelve sons, who each brought forth one of the twelve tribes of Israel. (Painting by A. Vacarro)

# The Israelites of the Old Testament

The Israelites of the Bible were one of many Semitic-speaking tribal groups in the ancient Near East. Their early history, as related in the Book of Genesis, takes place in Mesopotamia, Syria, present-day Israel and the Palestinian areas, and Egypt. The belief in one God is central to the religion of Israel and contrary to the pagan beliefs of the other ethnic groups in the ancient Near East. Special commitments called covenants were considered to be made between God (Yahweh) and the Israelites.

God spoke to Abraham, promising the Israelites a land of their own, and they moved to the land of Canaan. His grandson Jacob established the nation of Israel through his twelve sons (creating the twelve tribes of Israel), but hardship forced a move to Egypt. It was finally Moses who lead the Israelites out of their bondage. The Exodus from Egypt took them to the Sinai Peninsula, where Moses was given the Ten Commandments from God. These require obedience to His laws of proper behavior, in return for His leading them to the Promised Land. Moses, before his death, selected Joshua to make the final leg of this journey and lead the Israelites from Transjordan (Moab) to Canaan.

Throughout their time of struggle the God of the Israelites did not fail them, despite their occasional doubts, lapses in faith, and rebellions. God also instructed them to build a tabernacle (tent) as a special place of worship in which the box containing the Ten Commandments (ark of the covenant) would be placed. This solidified the Israelites' commitment to their God.

While the Bible tells of specific people and places in the lands where the Israelites traveled and settled, there are few comparable documents in the records of the civilizations of these areas. The most important is a stele of the Egyptian pharaoh Merneptah (thirteenth century BC). Pharaoh Merneptah was king of ancient Egypt, of the Nineteenth Dynasty. He was son and successor of Ramses II, and succeeded (1224 BC) to the throne when he was already advanced in years. He put down a rebellion in Syria and turned back a Libyan invasion of the Nile Delta on the western side. The first recorded mention of the tribal name of Israel was found in an inscription on the stele of Merneptah showing his pleasure in having achieved a military victory in a campaign in western Canaan. His reign was apparently

the beginning of the decline of Egypt, and after his death, a series of palace intrigues weakened the realm.

Samson at the destruction of the Temple, as described in the Book of Judges in the Bible. Flemish tapestry from the sixteenth century AD

Joseph with Potifar's wife on a painting by Tintoretto (sixteenth century AD). This woman, who was married to Joseph's boss, tried to tempt him. When he resisted, she accused him of seducing her.

Akhenaton's capital Akhetaton, in Tel el Amarna. In 1887 about forty tablets in Akkadian cuneiform were found there. The tablets consist of correspondence between royalty and rulers in Palestine and Syria, and they reveal much about ancient Egypt and the Middle East. The AD 1887 find of official government letters from fourteenth century BC Amarna shows that Egyptian control over Canaan was flagging under Pharaoh Akhenaton (1353–1335 BC). The Amarna correspondence offers many details in this regard. These messages, exchanged between the pharaoh and the rulers of the ancient Near East, were written on clay tablets in Mesopotamian cuneiform script and consisted of a series of complaints about the chaotic situation. Local governors, including the one in Jerusalem, accused one another of conspiring against the pharaoh. They begged the pharaoh to send troops: "If aid is forthcoming this year," the ruler of Jerusalem wrote, "the provinces of my lord master will be saved. If aid is not forthcoming, they will be destroyed."

### The Exodus

The man who would lead the Hebrews out of Egypt, freeing them from pharaonic oppression, was Moses. According to the Old Testament books of Exodus and Deuteronomy, he was born in Goshen, Egypt. His mother hid him in a basket made of papyrus and floated it on the river to save him from the pharaoh's order to put all Hebrew male infants to death (Exodus 2:4; Numbers 26:59). The pharaoh's daughter found and raised him.

As a foreigner with an illustrious career in the government service to Egypt, Moses witnessed an Egyptian overseer beat one of his fellow Hebrews, an event that would prove central to the history of his people. In a fit of rage, Moses killed the overseer and was consequently forced to flee the Egyptians' wrath. His office and commission were taken from him.

Moses fled to the Sinai Desert. There he encountered related Semitic groups who were still living the ancient nomadic life. Moses joined them, probably gaining a greater sense of his own identity and a desire to restore his people to the way of life of their ancestors, outside of Egypt. (He also married the daughter of a Midianite chief who bore him two children.) It was in the desert that Moses had his first visions of the God of Abraham, Isaac, and Jacob, called Yahweh. (The word *Jehovah*, used as a reference to the unnameable God, means "He who is.") When he was eighty (biblical) years old, Moses saw Yahweh in a burning bush, commanding him to return to Egypt and lead the Hebrews out of Egypt to Canaan.

Before Moses got to Egypt, he discussed his strategy with his brother Aaron, whom

certain but may have taken place in the thirteenth century BC, during the reign of Pharaoh Ramses II or that of Merneptah, his successor, if it is a historical fact. (Some contemporary historians assume that the stay in Egypt and the exodus from Egypt to Palestine are legends inspired by moral and theological considerations.)

### A People in the Desert
The journey from Egypt through the Sinai Desert took the Hebrews forty years according to the Bible. The journey was strenuous and full of hardship. At times, mass hysteria threatened to thwart Moses' plans. Under these circumstances, it is comprehensible that an entire people saw Mount Sinai burn, heard it roar, and shrank away in fright when trumpets and voices rang out. Perhaps the forty-year trek through the desert had another purpose—to rid the Hebrews of all Egyptian influences and to ban the last traces of superstition and idol worship. If so, the hardship the desert imposed was eminently suited to the goal. The prolonged contact with other desert-dwelling, Semitic nomads reinforced the identity of the people of Israel. In any case, the Exodus book of the Bible displays virtually no Egyptian influence. (This is unlike Mesopotamian and Syrian influence, which leaves numerous traces in the Bible.)

### The Ten Commandments
When the Hebrews reached the foot of Mount Sinai, on the Sinai Peninsula, Moses ascended the mountain. He spent forty days and nights with Yahweh, receiving from him two tablets of stone (or perhaps clay, like those used for cuneiform script) inscribed with what are called the Ten Commandments. (Moses would subsequently destroy the tablets in rage at the abandonment of their faith by his people, who were found worshiping a golden calf. Yahweh would then order him to carve and inscribe new ones, deposited in the Ark of the Covenant, the sacred place in the temple.)

Above all else, the commandments firmly established the concept of monotheism: "Thou shalt have no other gods before Me." Yahweh was the only god, unencumbered with goddesses and a pantheon of lesser gods, unlike the gods of the religions of other peoples in the area.

Exodus 20:1–17 and Deuteronomy 5:6–21 offer slightly different versions of the commandments, but the basic points are the same in both. The Exodus version gives a religious reason for observing the Sabbath, as against the humanitarian motive in Deuteronomy. The Exodus version also lists the wife with a man's possessions, in forbidding covetous-

Romanesque enamel from the twelfth century AD, portraying Moses and Aaron as the leaders of the Israelites on their journey through the desert.

Yahweh had sent ahead: "And Moses and Aaron went and assembled all the elders of the children of Israel. And Moses and Aaron spoke all the words that the Lord had spoken unto Moses, and did the signs in the sight of the people. And the people believed."

It took a lot more to convince the Egyptians to let the Israelites go. Ten plagues were required to accomplish this, but even then the pharaoh tried to stop them at the Red Sea. "Moses stretched out his arm, whereupon the Red Sea rose up in two walls, leaving dry land between them. The Hebrews crossed on the land, but when the Egyptians tried to pursue them, the walls of water broke upon them, and they drowned."

The date of the exodus from Egypt is not

ness, rather than according her a special place.

The Ten Commandments are grouped slightly differently in the various traditions that adhere to them: Jewish, Roman Catholic, Protestant, and Orthodox Christian. This is the customary Jewish version, considering the prologue as the first commandment and combining the next two as the second commandment:

1. The prologue: "I am the Lord thy God, who brought thee out of the land of Egypt, out of the house of bondage."
2. The prohibition of worship of any deity but God and prohibition of idolatry
3. The prohibition of the use of the name of God in vain
4. The observance of the Sabbath
5. Honoring one's parents
6. The prohibition of murder
7. The prohibition of adultery
8. The prohibition of stealing
9. The prohibition of giving false testimony
10. The prohibition of coveting (desiring) the property or the wife of one's neighbor.

Protestants and most Orthodox Christians combine the prologue with the first part of what is the second commandment here, prohibiting idolatry separately. Roman Catholics and Lutherans use St. Augustine's pattern from the fourth century AD, combining

Stained glass window made by a pupil of Hans Jacob Nuscheler (seventeenth century AD). The Israelites walk through the Red Sea, that opens up for them. The pharaoh's troops, in pursuit of them, are drowned.

View of Jordan, between Amman and Aqaba. This is the region in which the Israelites traveled on their way to the promised land after wandering in the desert.

323

Comb, dating from
the time that the Israelites settled
in Canaan
(second millennium BC)

the prologue and first two commandments, dividing the last into two.

The institution of the Sabbath and its name are of Mesopotamian origin. Observance of a day of rest probably existed as an ancient custom, later given religious significance.

Although the first five books of the Old Testament, called the Pentateuch, have been attributed to Moses, it is generally agreed that they represent the work of many authors. The Pentateuch is also called the Torah (Hebrew for "law" or "doctrine"). This refers to both the actual parchment scrolls on which the teachings are written, cherished in every synagogue, and to the oral Torah, the whole corpus of Jewish scripture and the historical commentary on it.

Moses died in the desert land of Moab. (Before he died, however, he turned the leadership of the people over to Joshua.) Forbidden to enter it, he was able to see Canaan, the Promised Land, from the top of Mount Pisgah (now in Jordan).

324   Moses has returned from Mount Sinai with the two tablets on which God's laws, the Ten Commandments, are written. Here, he explains them to the Israelites.

The battle between David and Goliath on a miniature in the Bible of the abbey of Colegiata de San Isidoro (León). On the right, the fight starts; on the left, young David cuts off the head of the heavily armed giant.

# Kings and Prophets

*The History of the Israelites until the Babylonian Exile*

After the death of Moses, the Israelites continued to reside on the eastern banks of the Jordan. On the other side of the river, the land of Canaan (Land of Milk and Honey) beckoned. According to the Book of Judges, "And Judah said unto Simeon his brother,

'Come up with me into my lot, that we may fight against the Canaanites.'

Judges presents a more probable historical account of the conquest of Canaan than the Book of Joshua, with its recounting of Joshua fording the Jordan and bringing down

The Canaanite
storm god Baal splits
the clouds with his
thunderbolt. With his
left hand he sticks a bolt
of lightning in the
ground. Stone relief
stele from Ugarit
(c.1700–1400 BC)

the walls of Jericho with trumpets. The occupation of the left bank of the Jordan probably took place gradually. Not all Israelites crossed the Jordan; quite a number of families stayed behind. Other nomadic tribes joined them on their trek to Canaan. The Bible calls them "descendants of Moses' father-in-law."

During the conquest, the newcomers profited from the internal strife among the Canaanites. The tribes of Manasseh and Ephraim rapidly moved to the mountainous north. The tribes of Benjamin, Simeon, and Judah settled in the south, between the Dead Sea and the coast. They encountered only the internally divided Semites and isolated Hittites. According to the Bible, Yahweh had ordered the eradication of the original population. However, although towns and villages were burned and the inhabitants killed, more often than not the native populace was left alone to coexist peacefully with the Israelites. The Jewish tribes particularly respected the Hittite villages, with their formidable reinforcements. According to the writings of later prophets, the mercy shown in the first phase of the conquest was the root of subsequent misery. It left the Canaanites free to practice their religion, which interested some of Yahweh's people.

## Baal and Yahweh

To the nomadic Israelites, settled Canaan was a land of luxury, including the exciting rites of the Canaanites. Israelites and Canaanites spoke related Semitic languages and were able to communicate with each other. Both facts combined to jeopardize the singular cult of Yahweh, which worshiped with sacrifice and piety.

The major gods worshiped in Canaan were Baal, a Canaanite deity, and the goddess Astarte or Ishtar, adopted from Mesopotamia by the Semites. Initially, Ishtar was depicted as the morning star. Later, she was considered the goddess of the waxing moon and the earth's fertility. She was often portrayed as the goddess of love (nude) or war (with weapons). Baal (literally the Lord) was a powerful storm god who demanded complete dedication from his servants. His rites were earthy, mystical, and exciting. Other Canaanite gods were fertility symbols who were seen as providing for rain and harvests.

The single God Yahweh appeared abruptly onto this variegated scene, the elements of his worship borne in the Ark of the Covenant. This sacred repository is described in Exodus 25 as a chest of acacia wood. Also referred to as the Ark of the Law, the Ark of the Testimony, or the Ark of God, it was two and a half cubits (3 feet, 9 inches or 1.5 meters) in length and one and a half cubits (2 feet, 3 inches or 70 centimeters) in width and height. The Israelites took it with them on military campaigns and carried it into battle on poles. It contained, according to various sources, Aaron's rod, a pot of

manna, and the stone tablets of the Decalogue (the Ten Commandments). In today's synagogues, the ark is still the place where the scrolls used in the worship service are kept.

The first Ark of the Covenant was set up at Shiloh, on the site of an earlier Canaanite sanctuary. The Israelites also worshiped Yahweh in Bethel, Gilgal, Mizpah, and Hebron. Canaanites soon built temples to Baal and Astarte next to the new Jewish sanctuar-

Saul, the first king of Israel, in a painting by Rembrandt (seventeenth century AD). The prophet Samuel anointed him as a king in the eleventh century BC.

Pottery from Canaan,
dating back to the early
to middle second
millennium BC

Stone stele from Shihan in Moab
(Transjordan) from the ninth to eighth
centuries BC, that may depict
one of the soldiers fighting the Israelites in
the area of Transjordan or represent
a warrior god with a spear.

ies. To many of the people of Israel, Yahweh now took on the aspects of a god of war.

## New Enemies and the Institution of the Monarchy

For more than a century, the Israelites lived in Canaan without a common leader. But when the old enemies—Canaanites and Hittites—united against a new power, they were forced to organize under one leader.

The new enemies were the Philistines. (The land Palestine derives its name from them.) At first, they only occupied five coastal towns: Gaza, Ashkelon, Ashdod, Ekron, and Gath. Before long, however, they began to drive the Israelites and Canaanites farther inland. The newcomers were not Semites. In all likelihood, they originated in the Mediterranean realm of the Minoan-Mycenaean culture and fled during the turmoil in the twelfth century BC. They were probably one of the "Sea Peoples" featured in Egyptian documents. Egyptian reliefs portray them as tall, slim warriors with narrow waists and feathered headdresses. In the Bible, the Philistines are also referred to as "the people of Kaftor" or "Kretim," perhaps referring to the island of Crete.

Samson, Gideon, Deborah, and Barakh are

legendary heroes of the transition from a tribal organization under chiefs, called judges, to the establishment of the Jewish monarchy. Now needing to choose a single ruler, the tribes crowned Abimelech, in Shechem, a king. His reign lasted only three years. The opposition he faced indicated that the tribes were not yet able to manage central rule.

The continuous raids by the Philistines, however, demanded political reorganization, especially when the Ark of the Covenant was seized by the Philistines during a battle. They restored the Ark to the Israelites when pestilence broke out in their ranks. (It was not returned to Shiloh immediately, causing great consternation among the priests there who had cared for it.) The priest Samuel anointed a man named Saul as king.

Control of the tribal chiefs had always been limited. The transition to a strong,

powerful monarchy was accompanied by great difficulty. The Bible is not very clear about the manner in which Saul was elected king or about the motivation behind his selection. It is even possible that Saul was anointed against his wishes. From the outset, his rule was not fully accepted. This forced him to fight enemies within his own society as well as outside it, and he met a tragic death. Run through with his own sword and abandoned, Saul died in battle against the Philistines on the plains of Gilboa.

### The Holy City of Jerusalem

Saul's successor, David, was also chosen by the priests of Yahweh. He set out to establish a capital for all the Israelites. For this purpose, he selected Jerusalem, an old Jebusite citadel in the mountains of Judaea. This is referred to as Uru-Salem ("City of Peace") in the Amarna Letters, an archaeological find

View of Jerusalem; the temple mount where Herod's temple used to stand. The prophets predicted the destruction of the city.

ΔΑΥΙΔ· ΓΟΛΙ ΑΘ ΑΛΑ ΖΟ ΝΕΙΑ

ΔΑΥΙΔ·

ΙCΡΑ ΗΛΙ ΤΑΙ

ΑΛΛο ΦΥ ΛΟΙ

ΓΟΛΙΑΘ

The fight between David and Goliath. In the upper half, Goliath throws his spear at David; in the bottom half, Goliath is defeated and killed by David.

of clay tablets in Egypt inscribed with the international diplomatic correspondence of the royalty of this era. He conquered the city in about 1000 BC and took the Ark of Yahweh there. He had created a new political and religious center far removed from the major trade routes along the Mediterranean. Jerusalem lay in an arid, hilly region, where the battle for survival hardened the people and where the temptations of luxury and idolatry were few. Perhaps David intended it that way to safeguard his own rule and his ties to Yahweh. Whatever the reason, the concept of Yahweh evolved in Jerusalem. He was no longer considered a warlike, tribal god but a universal, merciful one.

The center of ancient Jerusalem, called "the city of David" or Zion, consisted of two hills separated by a ravine. Traditionally, the major portion of the populace lived on the western hill. The religious buildings lay on

## The Book of Judges

The biblical Book of Judges details a battle between the Israelites and the Philistines, who wanted to expand their power farther inland, encroaching on the Israelites and Canaanites from the five coastal cities they controlled. The Israelites were commanded by local judges, who were accorded military powers in times of danger. The Bible lists twelve judges, including Gideon, Jephtah, and Samson, between c.1200 and 1025 BC.

Samson probably served as a judge for some twenty years. In accordance with the commandment of Yahweh, Samson had been sworn in as a Nazarean. This meant that he was not permitted to drink wine during his entire life and that he had to let his hair and beard grow.

Three Philistine women played a major role in Samson's heroic deeds. The first story tells how Samson weds a Philistine woman from the town of Timna. During the wedding banquet, he tells some Philistines a riddle and promises them thirty tunics and vestments if they solve it. His new wife gives the Philistines the answer. Enraged at her disloyalty, Samson kills thirty Philistines to pay his debt. He then returns to the house of his father, but the thought of the beautiful Philistine woman continues to tempt him. When he finally decides to fetch her, she had been married off to another Philistine. For revenge, Samson catches three hundred foxes and ties them by the tails in pairs. He lights torches between them and chases the animals through the Philistine fields. The Philistines subsequently wreak their revenge by burning Samson's wife and her father alive. As the battle rages, Samson kills more than a thousand of the enemy with the jawbone of an ass.

The second story unfolds during a visit by Samson to the city of Gaza. While he rests in the arms of a harlot, the Philistines lock the gates of the city and lay an ambush. Samson awakens, tears the city gate from its hinges, and carries it on his back to a mountain near Hebron.

In the third story, Samson falls in love

with the sensuous Delilah. This beautiful woman prefers the money offered by the Philistine kings. She promises to find out the secret of Samson's strength and to betray him to them. She continues to bother Samson with her questions and finally he tells her his strength resides in his long locks. Delilah then puts him to sleep, cuts his hair, and delivers him to the Philistines, who put out his eyes. He works in Gaza as a slave on the millstone. During a celebration in honor of the god Dagon he is put on public display. The blind giant then prays that Yahweh will restore his strength one more time. He does. Samson pushes the two pillars he was chained to apart. He and three thousand Philistines perish in the ruins of the building.

The stories appear as propaganda to encourage the Israelites against the expansionist Philistines.

Head of the god Baal, who was worshiped by the Canaanites. It was found in Aleppo. First millennium BC

While Samson is sleeping, Delilah cuts his hair. This made him powerless, for his strength was in his long hair. As soon as he woke up, Delilah handed him over to his enemies, the Philistines. (Painting by Andrea Mantegna, late fifteenth century AD)

Solomon, who ruled
Israel after his father, David,
had died, carried on his
father's work. During his
reign, his country prospered
also because of the
decline in Egypt and Babylon.
Solomon married foreign
women, and started worshiping
their gods. (Painting by
Sebastian Conca, eighteenth
century AD)

the eastern hill, close to Jerusalem's only water source. This is where the Ark of Yahweh was kept, inside a tent within the royal chambers.

David ruled before Assyria had expanded its empire. He was a curious mixture of soldier, poet, and thinker, well acquainted with human frailty, as is frequently evident in biblical stories. Shortly before his death, he had expropriated the upper part of the eastern hill, called Mount Moria, with the intention of building a temple for Yahweh. Aided by Phoenician architects and craftsmen and with materials from Lebanon, his son Solomon conceived the plan, and built a splendid structure and a palace complex (c.966–926).

Solomon appears to have felt that trade was as important to the country as engaging in battle. He allied himself with the Phoenician king Hiram of Tyre, who sent a merchant fleet to Ophir (possibly present-day Somalia) every three years. Hiram sent sailors and shipbuilders, while Solomon provided the harbor of Elat (ancient Ezion-Geber) on the eastern arm of the Red Sea, conquered in David's reign, and also traded with Seba (probably southern Arabia). The

arrangement enabled Solomon to procure the means to maintain a magnificent court.

Following his death, the monarchy divided into two hostile principalities. The warlike tribes in the northern kingdom of Israel were fed up with the luxurious monarchy of the House of David. Jeroboam first founded a new capital in Shechem, to be superseded ultimately by Samaria. The tribes of Judah and Benjamin in the south remained loyal to Rehoboam (Solomon's son) and his successors and maintained Jerusalem as their capital.

Decline was rapid. The sanctuaries of the northern tribes were established at Dan and Bethel. It was not long until Bethel was filled with images of Baal and Astarte. The temple in Jerusalem was also desecrated. The degree to which idolatry had progressed is clear in a passage from the time of King Josiah: "And the king commanded to bring forth out of the temple all the vessels that were made for Baal and for Astarte and to burn them at the brook Kidron. And he brought out the image of Astarte from the house of the Lord. And he broke down the houses of the Sodomites that were in the house of the Lord and those of the women

The prophet Elijah in a fifteenth-century Byzantine painting. The Book of Kings in the Bible tells the story of his life.

that wove coverings for Astarte; and he took away the horses given to the sun at the entrance of the house of the Lord; and he burned the chariots of the sun with fire" (2 Kings 23: 4–11).

## The Prophets

Angry prophets criticized the kings of Judah and Israel for their misdeeds. The Israelites called them *nabis*, meaning "he who speaks." They became known by their Greek name of prophet or "he who speaks in the name of another." The "other" referred to here was Yahweh. How could Yahweh, the prophets asked, the Almighty God who had defeated Israel's enemies, now tolerate so much unfaithfulness and abuse?

The first man attempting to publicly answer the question was Amos, a shepherd from the region around Jerusalem. On a holy day around 760 BC, he went to the sanctuary at Bethel, where he held forth in a rage, uttering terrible threats to those who had turned away from Yahweh. The simple shepherd boldly addressed the priest Amaziah and uttered the following threats to his face: "Your wife shall commit adultery in the city, your sons and your daughters shall be slain by the sword, your land shall be divided by the yardstick, you shall die on unclean soil . . . I detest your feasts, and cannot bear your gatherings. Yes, when you bring me burnt offerings and your offerings of food, I do not take pleasure in them, and your peace offering of fatted calves I do not wish to behold. Keep from me the roar of your songs, I do not wish to hear the strum of your harps. . . . so sayeth the Lord."

According to Amos, the people of Israel would be destroyed and dispersed, their children would be mistreated and sold as slaves. This raised the question of why Yahweh would only punish the second generation. Another prophet, Hosea, postulated an

The priests of the god Baal watch the offer of the prophet Elijah accepted by the real God. This stained-glass window was made by one of Hans Jacob Nuscheler's pupils (seventeenth century AD).

333

Two Assyrian soldiers lead two chariot horses by their bridles. The Israelites had to be alert all the time because of Assyrian war threats. Eighth-century BC stone relief

Detail of a portable altar, depicting the prophet Isaiah. He is considered the greatest prophet because of his explicit preaching of the coming of the Messiah. Enamel by Eilbertus of Hildesheim (1150–1160 AD)

answer. Yahweh would not punish his people because he loved them despite their sins. To clarify this truth to the people, Hosea drew the metaphor of a man married to a harlot who kept on loving her despite her unfaithfulness. Yet Yahweh's patience, Hosea said, was nearly exhausted. He warned that if the people did not mend their ways, Yahweh would take away their land.

The prophets presented a concept of their God holding an entire people responsible for the sins of its individuals. If one person acted wrongfully, it was the result of lack of piety on the part of the majority. The notion of an impending fall of Israel evolved with the prophets. Yahweh's wrath was seen to manifest itself in the growing threat from the Assyrian Empire. Nineveh was seen to be Yahweh's instrument of revenge. In fact, beginning about 745 BC, Assyrian armies appeared at frequent intervals in Syria, Phoenicia, and Palestine (Philistia).

### Isaiah: A Character

During the anxious years of the late eighth century BC, the prophet Isaiah began speaking in Jerusalem. He wore the clothes of a penitent, walked with signs on his back, and appeared naked in the streets to point to the starkness of the imminent exile. Isaiah also added a new element to his prophecies: hope.

"Even if thy sins were red as scarlet, they will become white as snow; if they were red as crimson, they will become white as wool. If thou art willing and listen, thou shalt eat the good of the land; but if thou refuses and art defiant, thou shalt be slain by the sword, for the mouth of the Lord has thus spoken."

In 722 BC Samaria, the capital of the northern kingdom of Israel, fell. The Assyrian armies led thousands of Samarians into exile. The twenty-five-year-old Hezekiah ascended David's throne. The new king was a personal friend of Isaiah. Influenced by the prophet, he attempted to achieve a reconciliation with Yahweh. His first deed was to clean the temple in Jerusalem.

About 701 BC, the Assyrian king Sennacherib led his armies into Palestine and Levant. He laid siege to the city of Lachish and had his troops destroy it and the towns and villages of Judah. Jerusalem, overrun by refugees, put up a desperate defense. Sennacherib sent negotiators to Hezekiah to point out the untenable situation and demand his surrender. The negotiators cried to the king and the people who had gathered on the walls. Isaiah had counseled Hezekiah not to give in to the Assyrian demands. His prophecy came true, when a pestilence suddenly broke out in the Assyrian military camp. Sennacherib was forced to return to Nineveh. The people rejoiced. The prophecy of an inevitable fall appeared forgotten as Isaiah, the prophet of numerous calamities, rejoiced as well.

**A New Prophet and the Fall of Jerusalem**
Another prophet, a contemporary of Isaiah, predicted: "And Yahweh shall subjugate the nations of faraway lands and the swords shall be forged into scythes and the lances into plowshares. No nation shall war against another; and war shall no longer be seen on earth." His name was Jeremiah.

In the period of peace following Sennacherib's retreat, Yahweh was credited for the miraculous liberation. Jeremiah was

The prophet Jeremiah, painted on an altarpiece. He not only predicted the coming of the Messiah, but also the fall of Jerusalem.

Lebanon

Berytos
(Beirut)

PHOENICIANS

Syria (Aram)

Sidon

• Damascus

MEDITERRANEAN SEA

Tyros •

Israel

JORDAN
RIVER

• Samaria

Ammon

Jericho •

PHILISTINES

• Jerusalem

Betlehem

Gaza •

Hebron

DEAD SEA

Moab

Judaea

Negev Desert

Edom

Midian

ISRAELITES

The realm during the rule of king David
▬ (1005-965 BC ) and Salomo (965-925 BC )

The realms around 860 BC
⌐⌐ Judaea                          Phoenicians
▬ Israel                           Philistines
▬ Syria                            Ammon
▬▬ Southern border of
the Assyrian Empire 721 BC

The realms between 721 and 587 BC
☐ Judaea                          Moab
☐ Edom                            Ammon

Palestine from the arrival
of the Israelites until the time
of Persian rule

ken solely on Yahweh's orders.

Jeremiah also began to resist the policies of the king and his servants. They believed in the value of an alliance with Egypt to offer a defense against Assyria. Jeremiah was of the opinion that Egypt was no more than "a broken reed." One day he showed himself in the street carrying a yoke on his shoulders, predicting that soon all residents of Jerusalem would carry one. He was locked up again, but his voice could be heard. Baruch smuggled out his prophecies from prison. The king himself burned a scroll of his words, but the prophet turned out to have been right. In 586 BC, Jerusalem was seized by the armies of the Babylonian king Nebuchadnezzar and destroyed. He had already humiliated Assyria. The Book of Jeremiah closes with the following:

"The king of Babel slew the sons of Zedekiah before his eyes in Ribla; the king of Babel also slew all the princes of Judah; and he put out the eyes of Zedekiah; and the king of Babylon bound him in fetters and carried him to Babylon . . . and he burned the House of the Lord."

convinced that the situation would not last. He was sure Assyria would strike back and destroy the land. The stance he took was so unpopular that he was unable to appear openly. The last prophet before the Babylonian exile, he could neither read nor write. He dictated his prophecies to his aide Baruch, who read them in public. Jeremiah called the temple priests "swindlers" and the temple itself a "hiding place for robbers and thieves." The priests had him imprisoned a number of times. The Bible details the story of his trial. The priests demanded his death, but Jeremiah escaped by saying he had spo-

The remains of the Gate of the Sphinxes in the Hittite city of Alaça Huyük

# The Hittites

## *Powerful Rulers in Asia Minor*

The name of the Hittites, who flourished from 1600 to 1200 BC, often surfaces in the history of the Near East and Egypt. The great pharaoh Ramses II came close to defeat in the battle of Qadesh in Syria in 1285 BC against a Hittite army; in the end he concluded a peace treaty with them and married a Hittite princess. The exceptional pomp and circumstance used to celebrate this marriage indicate that a Hittite princess was a very prominent personage indeed. Later, Hittites are mentioned as both enemies and competi-

tors of the Israelites in Canaan.

Jerusalem and Hebron may have been Hittite colonies during the Iron Age. Even later, it is the Hittites once again who try to block the all-powerful and imperialistic Assyria. Hittite monarchs led large coalitions against Nineveh, in northern Mesopotamia. Only Shalmaneser III, in the ninth century BC, can boast of having forced the Hittites into paying tribute. In Assyrian and Egyptian sculptures the Hittites are portrayed as powerful men with flat foreheads,

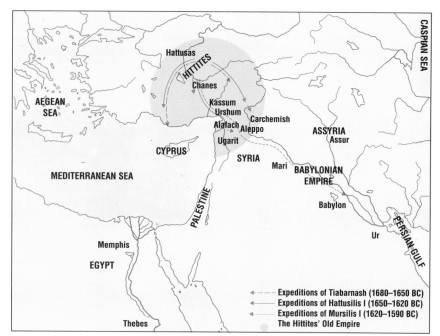

The Rise of the Hittite Empire

Expeditions of Tiabarnash (1680–1650 BC)
Expeditions of Hattusilis I (1650–1620 BC)
Expeditions of Mursilis I (1620–1590 BC)
The Hittites' Old Empire

slanted eyes, and hair hanging in braids down their backs. They vaguely resemble the later Turks and Mongols. Other Hittites, however, are pictured with different features, while some resemble Babylonians. We can assume that the various races in Asia Minor were mixed. The reigning upper classes were Indo-European in the second millennium BC.

The Egyptians gave the people we call Hittites the name *Khetta* and distinguished them from the inhabitants of Asia Minor and Syria as separate tribes. The Assyrian chronicles refer to them as *Hatti*. In the Bible they are indicated as the children of Heth, or the Hittites. However, the Greeks hardly knew of the existence of this unique tribe, perhaps the reason its existence was only recently taken seriously. The biblical references were considered to be allusions to a local tribe of Canaanites.

## On the Trail of the Hittites

This mighty people, the equal of Assyria and Egypt in their time, disappeared without leaving any trace other than a vague reference in the Bible. Much has been revealed through archaeological excavations, yet mysteries remain and there are many unanswered questions about Hittite civilization.

The center of Hittite power was in the central mountain area of Asia Minor. It is most probable that the Indo-European ancestors of the Hittites moved to Asia Minor across the Caucasus Mountains in approximately 2000 BC. From there they spread to the sea. The Hittites occupied the important strategic routes between Asia and Europe; their expansion to the south was through military

Bronze statuette of a man on horseback, made by the Hittites. It was found during the excavations in Boghazköy.

338

imperialism; they reached Syria and conquered Aleppo and Carchemish along the edges of the Euphrates River. They moved farther south in the Levant and reached the central area of Mesopotamia where they sacked Babylon in about 1595 BC.

When the Hittites finally settled in specific areas, they maintained much of their old feudal organization. During their war with Egypt, it looked like all power would end up in the hands of the "Great King" who lived in Hattusas–present-day Boghazköy. The ruins of this capital are located on the central plateau of Asia Minor and were excavated by several expeditions. Remnants of a palace and many temples were found, and great archives of documents were uncovered. The archives of the Great King consisted of approximately 20,000 clay tablets with cuneiform writing. They were written in Akkadian, the international language of diplomacy at the time, and Hittite. (Remarkably, in Hattusas no texts were found in Hittite hieroglyphic writing.) Some of the documents are copies of texts that were found in Egypt and match accurate Egypt diplomatic texts.

The oldest Hattusas texts date from the period of the late fourteenth century BC

when Mursilis II ascended the throne. Mursilis II was succeeded by his son Muwatallis, probably shortly after 1306 BC, who waged war against Pharaoh Sethi I and continued the war against Ramses II. Under Muwatallis the famous battle at Qadesh took place (1285 BC). The unsatisfactory end of this struggle resulted in Muwatallis being deposed and replaced by his brother Hattusilis III. He married his daughter off to the pharaoh and visited Egypt. The Hattusas documents delve deeply into these events

This stone lion was a gateway figure at one of the palaces in the city of Marash. It was made in the ninth century BC (Neo-Hittite).

Inscribed stone funerary stele of a priest, made by the Syrian Neo-Hittites. It originally comes from the region around Aleppo, an Aramaean kingdom (seventh century BC).

339

and report on Hattusilis's long reign. They continue until the reign of his grandson when the documents break off abruptly, perhaps because the capital was moved or overshadowed by Carchemish.

Hattusas was the capital of the Hittite Empire, the chief power and cultural force in Asia Minor, until about 1200 BC. The most famous Hittite rulers date from this period. Thereafter Carchemish was the most important Neo-Hittite kingdom in Syria. The town was situated along one of the three fords in the Euphrates and dominated the major trade route from Nineveh to the Mediterranean. The exact location of Carchemish was not identified until early in the twentieth century AD. On Assyrian reliefs, Carchemish is depicted as a city embraced by two arms of the Euphrates, a feature that made the city almost impregnable: Tuthmosis III of Egypt, Ashurnasirpal II, Shalmaneser III, and Tiglath-Pileser III of Assyria respectively attacked Carchemish but each had to give up. Only Sargon managed to conquer the Neo-Hittite city in 717 BC. In the meantime, because of its extensive trading contacts, Carchemish had imposed its system of weights and measures on the rest of Asia. No archives have been found in Carchemish, as they have been in Hattusas. Only the foundations of several large buildings were exposed during excavations sponsored by the British Museum. One of these may be the royal palace. The walls of this building had gates; on a relief the king can be seen supported by his son, the prince. It is possible that this represents the pronouncement of a new law. In the background is the royal family, eight children of various ages playing games, followed by the queen holding an infant and leading a musk ox.

The Neo-Hittite centers often employed a hieroglyphic writing of their own, in contrast to the north, where cuneiform writing was used in the second millennium BC. The Hittite hieroglyphic script contains signs that represent certain ideas such as king, city, and god, and signs that represent certain sounds. The lines must be read alternately from right to left and from left to right, the same way that the plow makes furrows in the earth. At the beginning of the twentieth century AD, the Czech scholar B. Hrozny discovered that a number of Hittite names were of Indo-European origin. He made great progress

Neo-Hittite stone relief from the ninth century BC with a picture of Teshup, the Hurrian storm god, who holds an ax and lightning in his hands.

with his knowledge of grammar and idiom and finally managed to decipher the texts written in cuneiform. The Hittite language is now accessible, but the hieroglyphs are still obscure. The greatest problem in deciphering the Hittite hieroglyphs is the scarcity of bilingual inscriptions. There is only one very short text in both hieroglyphs and cuneiform, on a seal of King Tarkudemmo. It reads: "Tarkudemmo king (of) city and country." This title also appears on the Hattusas clay tablets. The information contained on the seal of King Tarkudemmo consists of only six symbols. The first three indicate the name of the king, the others are titles. These six symbols are the only hieroglyphs that have been deciphered with certainty. Another obstacle to deciphering is the scarcity of texts. The hieroglyphs only came into use around 1000 BC, when the golden

Excavations in the trading city of Kanesh, near the village of Kültepe in modern Turkey

341

The postern gate and tunnel of Hattusas (near present-day Boghazköy). The walls are covered with reliefs depicting a procession of gods and important events in Hittite religion.

Terra-cotta vase, made in the eighteenth century BC. It was found during excavations in the city of Kültepe.

age of the Hittites had already passed, and they disappeared when Sargon of Assyria conquered Carchemish (717 BC).

## Culture and Ideology of the Hittites

The most important period of Hittite artistic development lasted from 1450 to 1200 BC, and drew upon much earlier sources from Sumer and Babylon, as well as upon local Anatolian (the area that is present-day western Turkey) influences from the third millennium BC. This was characterized by elaborate bronze and gold ornament. The pantheon of northern Syrian and Mesopotamian gods adopted by the Hittites were identified in Hittite art by the high pointed hats, short-skirted robes, and boots with long, curling toes on the males, and the long pleated robes and square hats of the females.

The Hittites were accomplished carvers and metalworkers. A particularly impressive late representation of deities, made to adorn a golden royal robe, is a series of ornaments from Carchemish carved in steatite and lapis lazuli, mounted in gold.

Animal figures are among the Hittite finds, but their main interest was in representing humans, particularly engaged in religious ritual. In one great sanctuary were discovered a magnificent series of mythological scenes carved in rock, depicting lions and sphinxes serving gods and goddesses.

The total absence of literary texts in the Hittite archives is remarkable. The only extant documents are peace treaties, letters about political matters, lists of kings, and religious texts. With these facts, we can partially reconstruct the history of the Hittites, but not their way of thinking. The only available work with literary value is a handbook

for taming horses. The writer of this book is a certain Kikkuli, who worked in the stables of Hattusas's court. His book describes in great detail, from day to day and from hour to hour, a method of taming wild horses that takes six months. It starts with selecting the best horses in a free-galloping herd. Then the chosen animals are made to fast and sweat to get rid of excess fat. The horses are even given emetics. When their strength is broken they are tamed and introduced to reins. Horse trading was an important activity of the Hittites.

Our knowledge of Hittite culture is derived to a great degree from archaeological excavations at several sites. One of the most

Bronze statue of a
Hittite god, made in the
sixteenth century BC

Detail of a basalt relief
with an inscription written
in Hittite hieroglyphs

# The Hittite Empire at Its Peak

In the remains of the Hittite capital of Hattusas, discovered near the Turkish town of Boghazköy in 1907, many historical documents were found which cast a light on the Hittite Empire at its peak. Written on approximately 10,000 baked clay tablets are accounts of military campaigns, treaties, coronations, and decrees. Each has an introductory historical analysis and most include commentary on anticipated future developments. These texts, unique to this culture, provide information essential to the reconstruction of the broad outlines of Hittite history.

Hattusas was founded in the middle of the seventeenth century BC by Hattusilis I, who fought repeatedly to defend the Hittites, especially against the Hurrians of Syria and the mountain people who lived near the coast of the Black Sea.

Under King Mursilis I, shortly after 1600 BC, attack and defense roles were reversed. The Hittites captured and destroyed the Syrian town of Aleppo and even sacked Babylon. Toward the end of the sixteenth century BC, conflicts within the royal families caused the rapid decline of this first empire. The rise of the New Kingdom in Egypt and of the Mitanni in northern Mesopotamia were serious threats to Hittite independence. In the fifteenth century BC, their legal code, one of the most lenient in antiquity, was based on restitution, not the retribution that was the norm elsewhere. They normally did not punish either by death or mutilation, both common in the ancient Middle East.

Around 1380 BC, Suppiluliumas founded the new Hittite state, basing it on strict military organization. During the early years of his reign, he had led an expedition against Damascus and had conquered several Syrian city-states. The use of several thousand war chariots enabled Suppiluliumas to conquer all of Syria.

His successors managed to keep the empire intact. They waged wars against the neighboring tribes, particularly Egypt, which, under the pharaohs of the Nineteenth Dynasty, was trying to stop Hittite expansion. During this period, Mursilis II fought against the mountain tribes in the north of his empire, and succeeded in subduing most of Asia Minor. His successor, Muwatallis II, fought against Pharaoh Ramses II at the battle of Qadesh in 1285 BC. The pharaoh claimed victory, but the Hittites probably won, since they subsequently controlled the area.

However, the battle against Egypt weakened the Hittite Empire on other fronts. The mountain tribes of Anatolia became increasingly dangerous in the thirteenth century. By the time Hattusilis III ended the wars with Egypt and concluded a peace treaty, it was already too late. Assyria loomed in the east. Toward the end of the thirteenth century BC, invaders known only as the Sea Peoples appeared, threatening the coasts of Asia Minor, Syria, and Egypt. In the turmoil, the city of Hattusas and the great Hittite Empire disappeared, probably as a result of a volcanic eruption in the Aegean that lead to famine and the migrations of peoples in the eastern Mediterranean area.

important is the capital, Hattusas, a huge site built on hills. The site is surrounded by a fortification wall with towers running for almost 4 miles (6 kilometers). Well-constructed buildings were made of large stone foundations with brick walls and wooden beams on top. In the Lower Town, the palace and the great temple of the god Hatti, the storm god of heaven, were found. The structure was surrounded by a complex of storerooms containing numerous large

storage jars. The Upper Town had no fewer than twenty-four temples which had bases for the statues of the gods.

Gateways to Hittite citadels often had elaborate stone sculptures in the form of guardian beasts. At Alaça Hüyük, there are sphinxes derived from the Egyptian type wearing a typical headdress, and lions were found at Hattusas.

The many storm gods have a similar look to them when represented in art. They wear short kilts with wide belts, tall helmets with horns, and hold battle axes and swords. Kings are dressed in long robes, caps, and hold a long curved staff, the symbol of their priestly role. Much of Hittite art is religious

Model of a firepot as they were used in the eighteenth century BC. The original was found in Kültepe.

Neo-Hittite relief stele depicting a priest who eats and drinks offerings and is assisted by a servant. Found near Aleppo, c. 600 BC

in nature and the king is often shown before a sacrificial altar or even in the protective embrace of a god.

Details of the king's role in religious ceremonies are found in the archives. The rites he performs in certain parts of the temple are reflected in the actual architectural plans of the temples found in the excavations. These include a special gate leading to the courtyard with a basin for ritual washing of his hands, and then into the sanctuary with a throne. In this building ritual meals were eaten, dedicated to the gods.

Perhaps the ancestors of the ancient Greeks—the Mycenaeans—had a few contacts with the Hittites. It is likely that the legends about the voyage of the Argonauts to the country of Colchis on the Black Sea and about Princess Medea who returned with them to Greece, hold a vague memory of Greek contact with territories that were part of the Hittite sphere of influence. Some scientists think that the legends about the Amazons, fearless female warriors, go back to such contacts, but this is very uncertain. Again, accounts from Hittite sources about a country or an island named Ahhiyawa may indicate the Hittites had encountered the Achaioi, or Greeks, in the area of the Aegean Sea.

### Religious Cults

The Hattusas archives give details about the large pantheon of deities worshiped and religious cults with their ceremonies and hymns. The royal texts are always cosigned with the name of •the queen mother who may also have been the high priestess of the national faith. Reverence for the gods extended into the sphere of politics and war. In the treaty between Hattusilis III and Ramses II, for example, the peace agreement is signed in 1269 BC on behalf of eighteen Hittite gods.

The many mythological texts clarify the complex nature of the cults, some of which are derived and adapted from different cultures. A common theme to many of the myths is that of order and chaos and the related battles of the gods.

Early in the Old Hittite period there were myths derived from older traditional Hatti ones, including that of the cosmic battle of the serpent monster Illuyanka and a storm god. There are many storm gods and sun deities in this period as well. Later, during the empire period, other myths are adopted from the Hurrians who lived in Syria and Mesopotamia. Teshup the storm god, for instance, becomes the head of the Hittite pantheon of deities whose consort is Arinna, the sun goddess. Kumarbi, god of grain and the harvest, is the powerful rival of Teshup in the end.

Another text tells the story of the battles for power and kingship in heaven. Some deities are also adopted from Mesopotamian and Syrian religion, including Ishtar, goddess of war, who is called Shauska by the Hittites.

Nature deities, including those of mountains, rivers, and springs, were also important. At the impressive ravine sanctuary at Yazilikaya, there is a carved rock relief with a procession of seventy gods and goddesses. They wear tall headdresses and some are standing on the backs of animals sacred to them. Teshup, the chief deity, is at the head of the procession.

### Iron and Horses

The Hittites were probably the first people to use iron on a large scale, thus bringing in the Iron Age. Their immediate ancestors, or other Indo-European groups, had introduced the horse as a means of drawing war chariots in the Near Eastern world. Both these events had a tremendous influence on the history of mankind. Donkeys and wild onagers, an ancestor of the donkey, had long been the only animals harnessed to chariots, but at the height of their power the Hittites used horses instead. By 1500 BC, the Egyptian pharaohs also had a brigade of warriors whose chariots were drawn by horses or mules. The Greeks of Mycenae were also familiar with the chariot, which is mentioned in the works of Homer.

The Hittites also made noteworthy contributions to society. About a hundred tablets were found at Hattusas, which together form a kind of civil code. They were probably written about 1500 BC.

These tablets show that Hittite society knew only two kinds of people: aristocrats and slaves or serfs. A middle class of rich citizens and merchants, which we find, for example, in Mesopotamia, is completely absent here. At a wedding among aristocratic landowners, the husband gives his bride a big dowry, which is kept by the parents of the bride. In case of divorce, the husband receives his money back. When the husband dies, his brother must marry the widow, whether or not he already has a wife. We also find this unusual requirement in the Israelite laws. In addition there are regulations for the transfer of property, which had to take place

So-called Lebanese mountain figure holding a spear, early second millennium BC, made of bronze

in the presence of a priest-notary. The return of an escaped slave was rewarded. There are also Hittite price lists. The prices are relative. If a mule is sold for one amount, a tamed horse costs twenty times as much and an ox fifteen times as much. A field on a farm has twenty times the value of a vineyard. The wages of educated workers are double those of forced laborers and slaves. Curiously enough, there are only eight crimes punishable by death. Usually the nose or ears are cut off instead. A murder committed outside the city is punished more severely, because in the countryside, there is less chance that a victim's cries for help will attract the attention of other people. This civil code shows us the other, practical side of the Hittites.

Music and dance probably reached a high level among the later Hittites; both were necessary for their celebrations. The reliefs of Carchemish show dances by veteran soldiers who wear animal skins and hide their faces behind masks. Displays of cruelties and atrocities—such as we see in neighboring Assyria—are completely absent. The reliefs in the palace of Carchemish also show idyllic scenes. We see the king speaking, with his hand resting on the shoulder of the vizier. A queen carries a small prince on her arm, who holds a rope in his little hands tied to a tame musk ox. The Neo-Hittite reliefs stand out because of their simple but warm humanity.

Bronze standard with openwork grill design dating from the late third millennium BC. It was found in an Alaça Huyük tomb.

Vessel in the shape of a lion. It was used for pouring ritual drink offerings. Red polished ware from Kültepe

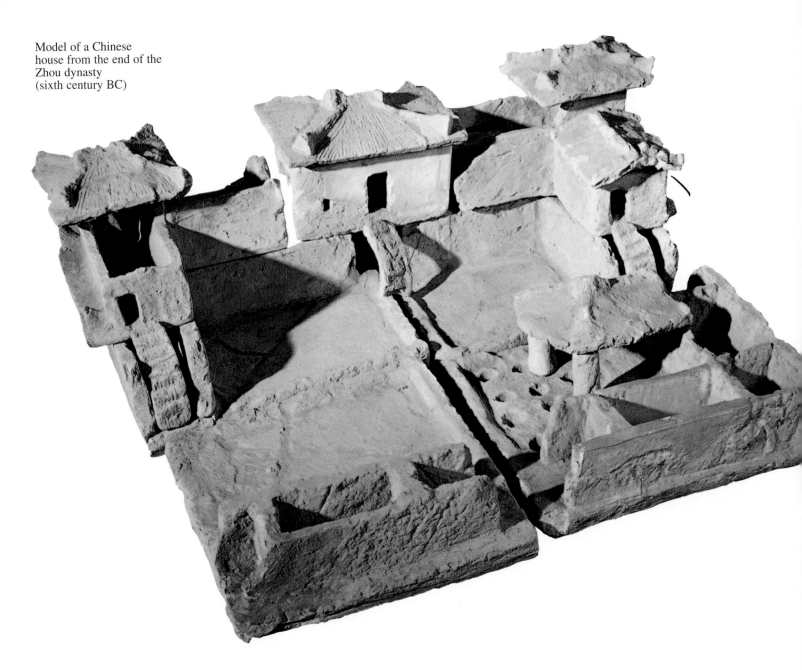

Model of a Chinese
house from the end of the
Zhou dynasty
(sixth century BC)

# The Early History of China

*From the Bronze Age to the Han Dynasty*

There is an ongoing debate as to when the
first people appeared in China. One view is
that an early hominid, *Homo erectus*, originated in Africa and moved from there
throughout the world, including to China.
Remains of Homo erectus, found near
Beijing, have been dated back 460,000
years. In conflict with this theory is the
notion that an independent development of
humans took place in Asia, probably in the
Huang He (Yellow River) Valley.

**Yang-shao Culture**
The Neolithic culture of the Yang-shao originated in western China about 3950 BC and
developed through 1700 BC. Evidence of
people practicing slash-and-burn agriculture
has been found in Shanxi and Henan. They
lived in wattle-and-daub homes in semiper-
manent groups and cultivated millet, wheat,
and silkworms. Hunters and fishers who
made use of specialized and polished stone
tools, they also kept pigs, dogs, some cattle,

349

sheep, and goats. They made pottery without a potter's wheel and painted it red, white, and black.

## Lung-shan Culture

The later Lung-shan (2000–1850 BC) of northern China may have derived from the Yang-shao but are usually considered independent. Other than the fact that their villages appear to have been more permanent and were surrounded by mud walls, much of their culture was similar. They made fine black pottery, also without a wheel, and practiced fortune-telling through the interpretation of bones (scapulimancy).

## The Xinjiang Mummies

Wang Binghua, China's top archaeologist, has been unearthing mummies with blond hair and Caucasian features in northwest China since 1978. Preserved solely by their burial in the hot stony soil between the

A tripod, called *li*,
made of clay dating from
the Neolithic period
(between c.4000
and 2500 BC)

Clay vase from the
New Stone Age (Neolithic
period), made in
the province of Gansu

Celestial Mountains (Tian Shan) and the Taklimakan Desert, they date from 2000 BC to 300 BC. Over a hundred have been found in four burial sites, raising questions as to the role of foreigners in the development of Chinese civilization. Wagon wheels, made of three carved boards fastened with dowels, have been found with the bodies. These are virtually identical to wheels made in the Ukraine, on the plains of Europe.

**Neolithic Farmers**

From 7000 BC on, Stone Age people began to farm in at least two areas of China. Characteristics of their cultures would develop at about 5000 BC, taking the first steps toward a more complex society. The dry, loamy soil north of the Huang-p'u River was ideal for growing the hard, nutritious grain called millet. People north of the Ch'inling Mountains and the Huai River began raising pigs, as well. In the warm, humid south, other people began wet rice farming and the raising of pigs and water buffalo.

By about 2000 BC, Chinese people were using lime plaster on their houses, making pottery, and carving jade and ivory. Some had developed metallurgical techniques for the working of copper. Along the Huang-p'u, bronze objects were being manufactured. Various groups exchanged goods frequently.

Groups also fought each other. Evidence of violence can be found in the increase in weaponry, the creation of ramparts around settlements, and the remains of those who died unnatural deaths. Clay platforms have been found within those settlements, as well, built to support the large buildings erected by those rich or powerful enough to mobilize a work force. The same elite group of citizens added the practice of human sacrifice to that of animal sacrifice. The same class created a system of oracles using animal bones and tortoiseshells that were scorched, and then had heated bronze sticks applied to them. The resultant cracks were then interpreted for meaning.

**The Shang Dynasty (c.1600–1050 BC)**

The Shang dynasty reigned in north central China, making its capital at Anyang about 1384 BC. Its economy was agricultural, based on millet, wheat, barley, and perhaps some rice. The Shang cultivated silkworms and raised dogs, pigs, sheep, and oxen. Urbanization had begun at that time, and the Shang was a culture of cities. A monumental architectural find of palaces, temples, and graves was found in and near those cities. The Shang used wood, clay, and thatch for construction. They produced bronze vessels, tools, and weapons, often lavishly decorated.

There is more information about the late Shang state (c.1250–1050 BC) than about the early, due to the survival of written texts, using over 2,000 characters. The Shang society was aristocratic and hierarchical, headed by a hereditary monarch.

His subjects, farmers for the most part, still lived in a Stone Age fashion. They used wooden spades and stone sickles. Their

earthenware was rough, while their masters' was delicate and beautifully decorated. The rulers appointed by the king were the masters of the farms, the landed estates, and the villages surrounding the cities.

A literate priestly class, neither aristocrats nor commoners, were responsible for administrative records and matters of religion. The priests were expected to divine the future by interpreting oracles of bone and to provide advice from a pantheon of gods headed by

*Ting*, a bronze sacrificial vessel for food, made during the Shang dynasty. It was used for preparing food during offering ceremonies.

A *you*, a bronze
wine container that was
made during the
Shang dynasty

Bronze halberd
from the Shang dynasty,
decorated with sheep
heads

Shang Ti (the Lord on High). The Shang people worshiped their ancestors as well as their gods, sacrificing animals and humans to them.

### Anyang

In 1927, the first sod was cut for archaeological research near the city of Anyang. Almost immediately, beautiful bronzes were discovered, dating from the late Shang period (1250–1050 BC). The wealth of bronze gave evidence that Anyang had been a very important city. It stretched along the Huan River, a tributary of the Huang-p'u, for 3.6 miles (5.8 kilometers), and included a string of royal graves, palace and temple complexes, and residential and industrial areas.

The royal graves have almost all been plundered, but out of the one intact burial site left, an immense wealth of bronzes and jades has been recovered. Some two hundred pieces of ritual vessels were found in the grave of Fuhao, possibly the wife of a Shang king. The power and prosperity of those buried at Anyang can also be determined from the very large size of the graves and from the numbers of people and animals (monkeys, deer, horses, and even elephants) sacrificed during the burial ceremonies. The oldest chariots in China are found there.

The oracle bones found at Anyang were particularly important because during the Shang dynasty the questions posed and answers received were recorded on the bones for the first time, making them a form of early historical texts.

### The Chou Dynasty (c.1050–256 BC)

The people of Chou lived in the valley of the Wei River, toward the far western part of China. They belonged to a different ethnic group than the Shang, although they shared the same bronze culture.

According to traditional historiography, the Chou rulers made subjects of the Shang in c.1050 BC. The traditional Chinese explanation describes the last Shang king as a degenerate monster whose deposition by a count from western China was "what Heaven wanted." The Shang's mandate from Heaven had been passed on to the Chou. Such a justification for the taking of power had already been offered for the Hsia-Shang transition. This would remain the typical, if propagandistic, explanation of dynastic succession for much of China's long history.

The Chou ruled most of northern China, including the Yangtze River. Their domain was so extensive and communication so limited that they delegated administration to vassals, making their positions hereditary. Each lord ruled from a walled town over designated territory that he controlled with his own military. The territory to be farmed was divided into squares of nine plots each. Individual peasant families worked the outer eight tracts, collectively farming the center tract for the lord. Below them in social rank were domestic slaves.

The lords in each state were nominally subordinate to the dynastic king, who was said to rule by a mandate from Heaven. In reality, however, they became more powerful than the king, frequently warring with each other and seizing territory. Through a process of consolidation, the states became larger, fewer, and increasingly autonomous, forcing the king to share real power with the lords until the king was merely a symbolic head of these states.

States on the periphery of China forged alliances with non-Chinese. In 770 BC, a coalition of states and non-Chinese allies drove the Chou to establish a new capital to the east, at Loyang. Called the Eastern Chou, they had little control over their still-nominal vassal states.

The militaristic states replaced the chariot, once central to the conduct of war, now a means of luxurious transportation, with infantry. By the fifth century BC, they added cavalry (a concept learned from non-Chinese) to the infantry. From the sixth century onward, war was no longer the aristocratic affair it had been. The infantry comprised farmers, put under increasingly direct

A more ornately ⟩
decorated *you*, also of
bronze

353

control even when they were not mobilized. The infantry, and eventually the cavalry, became indispensable against the recurring invasions from north and west that increased in the fourth century, when steppe nomads attacked the sedentary Chinese farmers time and again.

As defense against the barbarian raids, the Chou built "long walls," usually of clay, at their northern and western borders. As defense against each other, they built walls between the various states as early as the

Bronze container
from the beginning of the
Zhou dynasty
(sixth century BC)

seventh century BC. They also built interstate alliances. These offered some means of political stability as the Chou dynasty declined over the seventh and sixth centuries BC, but by the late fifth century BC, most of these alliances had failed. A period of warfare and anarchy ensued in 403 BC, an era that overlapped with the closing years of the Chou and came to be known as the Period of the Warring States. The Chou collapsed toward the end of it, in 256 BC, and yet it was also a period of enormous significance in Chinese economic and intellectual development.

Bronze buckle that is
inlaid with pieces of jade.
It was made at the end of the
Zhou dynasty (fourth to
third centuries BC)

# The Great Rivers of China

The Yangtze, or Chang Jiang (also Ch'ang Chiang), is the longest river in China and Asia, running some 3,400 miles (5,470 kilometers) from the Kunlun Mountains (at an elevation of about 16,000 feet or 4,877 meters) in southwest Qinghai (Tsinghai) Province south through Sichuan (Szechwan) Province into Yunnan (Yün-nan) Province, then northeast and east across central China to the East China Sea, just north of Shanghai. The Chinese name for the entire river is Chang Jiang (Chang Kiang), or "Long River." In China, it is only called the Yangtze for about the last 400 miles (644 kilometers) of its course, where it flows through the region of the tenth-century BC Yang kingdom.

Most of the Yangtze offers a huge network for transportation and communication. Navigable by seagoing ships for 600 miles (965 kilometers) and by river steamers for 1,000 miles (1,609 kilometers), its passage for 200 miles (322 kilometers) through the Yangtze Gorges is perilous for boats. The river drains over 650,000 square miles (1,683,500 square kilometers) of China through its numerous tributaries. Its main branches are the Han, Yalong (Ya-lung), Jialing (Chia-ling), Min, Tuo He (T'o Ho), Wu, and Huang He (Huang Ho), also called the Yellow River.

Two thousand years ago, Emperor Yang-ti had the Grand Canal (Da Yunhe) dug, joining the Yangtze to the Yellow River as a means of flood control. Starting at Zhenjiang (Chinkiang), it is the longest canal in the world (1,000 miles or 1,609 kilometers) and still provides that function. Lakes Dongting (Tung-t'ing) and Poyang (P'o-yang) also take overflow from the Yangtze in the rainy season. Despite this, devastating floods still occur, most recently in 1980 and 1981.

The Yellow River gets its name from the large quantity of yellow clay it carries. This

The Yangzijiang/ Yangzi River, one of the two most important rivers of China

clay or silt is loess, a fertile loam, carried by wind as well as water. Each flooding of the river leaves a layer of loess on the land, adding to its fertility. The Yangtze deposits more than 6 billion cubic feet (168 million cubic meters) of silt annually in Jiangsu Province alone, making it a major region of rice production. Chinese civilization, linked to agriculture, originated in the great river valleys. They remain the most populous and economically vital areas in China.

## The Period of the Warring States (c.500–221 BC)

Despite the political situation, the late Chou era was prosperous. The population grew. Agriculture expanded and was intensified, largely owing to irrigation works. Commerce and urbanization developed. The use of iron, first introduced around 500 BC, became commonplace. A market economy based on coins developed. Government was given a solid foundation as the first laws of China were written. A highly developed administrative system allowed governments to undertake enormous public works, like the construction and maintenance of river dikes, the building of irrigation works, and the digging of canals. On the other hand, farmers were the victims of the violence of war,

Statue of a horseman from the army of Qin

whether soldiers or noncombatants. They had to pay exorbitant taxes, they were devastated by flooding and epidemics, and they had to sell their children in time of famine. Many were forced into labor, called upon for such work as the construction of an ostentatious grave for a member of the elite.

## Classical Age of Chinese Philosophy (1027–256 BC)

During the late years of the Chou dynasty, despite the political turmoil (or because of it), several philosophies developed in China that would influence the world. Known as the Five Classics and the Four Books, they were all written in this era and all relate to Confucianism: *The Changes, The Writings of Old, The Poems, I li (The Ceremonials),* and *The Spring and Autumn Annals; Lun yu (The Sayings of Confucius), Mencius, The Doctrine of the Mean,* and *The Great Learning.*

### Confucius (551– 479 BC)

The society Confucius was born into was patriarchal, its organization feudal. Service to the government, not individual initiative, was sanctioned. Within the government, all records were maintained by a highly competitive literate elite. The focus of all educa-

A decorative jade slab made at the end of the Zhou dynasty (third century BC)

tion was preparation for government work. Heaven, or the sky, was said to be the great overseer of the government.

The K'ung family that Confucius was born into was poor but noble. His father was a minor bureaucrat in the feudal state of Lu, on the Shantung Peninsula. An advisor to state leaders, Confucius' philosophy won him the title *K'ung Fu-tzu* (Grand Master K'ung); in Latin, Confucius. In turbulent times he sought order, internal and external, through personal right conduct and tradition, harking back to an ideal society exemplified in antiquity. "When the personal life is cultivated, the family will be regulated; when the family is regulated, the state will be in order; and when that state is in order, there will be peace throughout the world."

Individuals, he said, should lead virtuous lives following the example set by their leaders: "He who exercises government by means of his virtue may be compared to the north polar star, which keeps its place, and all the stars turn toward it."

### Mencius (c.371–c.289 BC)
His disciple Mencius took the duty of the ruler to the people a step further. Believing people inherently good, he insisted that government be exercised on their behalf. When it was not, subjects had the right to depose it.

If rebellion occurred against a king, ruling by mandate from Heaven, it only indicated that Heaven had withdrawn the mandate. Mencius was one of the followers responsible for the spread of Confucianism to the point where it was elevated to a state ideology during the Han dynasty (206 BC–AD 220).

### Lao-tzu (c.570–c.490 BC)
The sage Lao-tzu, a contemporary of Confucius, sought *Tao* (the way) in nature rather than in society. He examined nature to understand man, focusing on personal growth. *The Tao Te Ching (Classic of the Way and Virtue)*, explaining his philosophy, is attributed to him by tradition, although it may have been recorded by his students from things he said. In it, people are asked to go with the flow of nature, a nonaction called *wu-wei*. Lao-tzu emphasized a return to simple agrarian life, a life not regulated by government.

### Hsün-tzu (c.298–c.230 BC)
The Confucian Hsün-tzu disagreed, contending that humans, by nature evil, required explicit controls to regulate their conduct. He did allow room for human improvement through education (the study of the classics of the past) and social regulation.

A tiger attacks a wild goat. Metal plaque from the time of the Zhou dynasty (sixth century BC)

No doubt one of the most spectacular archaeological finds of the last decades is this great collection of terracotta statues, found in 1974 near the grave of the first Chinese emperor.
The statues, probably lifelike portrayals of all the soldiers in his army, are all life-size and very detailed.
Incredibly enough, they all surfaced in very good condition.

### Han-fei-tzu (d. 233 BC) and Li Ssu (c.280–208 BC)

Han-fei-tzu and Li Ssu expanded the views of Hsün-tzu into the philosophy of legalism, putting their emphasis on control of human nature and punishment of wrong behavior. Legalism assumed that strict enforcement of a predetermined set of regulations, in accordance with specific penalties for violations, would result in the efficient management of society. The subordination of personal freedom to authority became the dominant philosophy of the next dynasty, the totalitarian Ch'in.

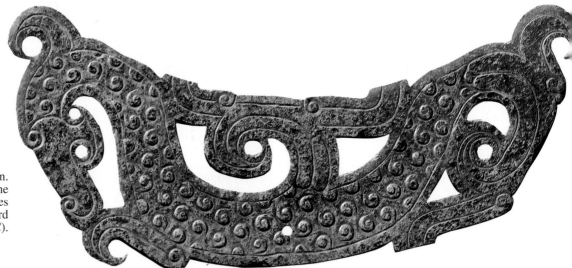

Image of a dragon. It dates from the period of the Warring States (early fifth to late third century BC).

## The Ch'in Dynasty (221–206 BC)

In 221 BC, the northwestern feudal state of Ch'in gained the royal power the Chinese states had fought over since 500 BC. Its king declared himself *Shih Huang Ti*, or First Emperor of the Ch'in dynasty. The Chinese called their country either by the name of its ruling dynasty or *Chung-kuo*, the Middle Kingdom, reflecting their view of geography. But eventually a variation of the name *Ch'in* would be adopted by the rest of the world as a name for the whole country.

Ch'in, stronger and richer than the surrounding states, had directed all effort at effective government and successful war-

A stretch of the Great Wall of China in the mountains near Beijing. The construction of the wall was started in the third century BC, but the part in the picture dates from the sixteenth century AD.

359

making. A centralized government had replaced the semiautonomous feudal lords. Now, aided by a legalist minister, the First Emperor replaced the semiautonomous feudal states with a centralized administration. He abolished the hereditary aristocratic families, broke up their lands into provinces, and assigned bureaucrats to run them. He ended the practice of feudalism, encouraging private landholding. The situation of the farmers did not improve much. Those who now received the land as private property, officials among them, were members of the privileged classes. They controlled the system of

An oracle bone
that was used for predicting
the future in ancient
China

taxation, lobbying for influence at his court. The situation would breed rebellion.

The emperor began systematic work on the Great Wall, adding some 1,200 miles (1,930 kilometers) to it using forced labor, another cause for resentment. It was completed in 204 BC, with a combined length of 36,125 miles (58,125 kilometers).

The Ch'in administration promoted economic and social integration of the vast empire. Through mandated uniformity it standardized coinage, weights and measures, axle widths, and culture. It simplified char-

acter writing, developing the Simple Seal system and making its use compulsory. The emperor also attempted to standardize thinking. In 213 BC, he made legalism the state doctrine and ordered the books of all other philosophies burned.

Requiring military service of the peasants to people his armies, the emperor sent them south to the Yuan Hong (Red River) in today's Vietnam. He took control of the huge area covered by today's adjacent provinces of Sichuan, Yunnan, and Guizhou, and all of China north of the Yangtze River, even part of the Korean Peninsula.

The First Emperor's authority and organizational skills are apparent in his huge burial mound, .3 miles (483 meters) in diameter, near modern Xian. In its vicinity, a buried terra-cotta army was discovered in 1974, comprising thousands of life-size statues of soldiers and horses.

Yet the new empire remained in the hands of its founding family only fifteen years, testimony to the fact that its basic principle, legalism, had gained no general acceptance. With the death of the First Emperor, the people rebelled. In 206 BC, a rebel army officer of nonaristocratic birth proclaimed the new Han dynasty (206 BC–AD 220). It would retain the centralized system of state administration of the Ch'in but would reject most other aspects of legalism. (The Ch'in-style hierarchy of administration lasted until AD 1912.) The Han government turned to Confucianism as the underlying philosophy of the vast bureaucracy it developed to organize and control its empire.

### The Oracle-bone Inscriptions

Chinese writing uses a single character for every word. There are over 40,000 characters. Some 3,000 of them have been identified from the Shang dynasty, incised on tortoiseshells and the sheep and cattle scapulae (shoulder blades) that were used as oracles. About 800 of these have been deciphered with certainty. Found by the tens of thousands, these oracular writings are the oldest texts in the language.

Chinese writing has since changed, but its principles and many symbols have not. Originally picture writing, Chinese builds on hundreds of single pictographs for basic words and hundreds more compound pictographs for more complex words. Spoken Chinese, consisting of more abstract words, is still linked to the same pronunciation heard 3,000 years ago.

# The Persians

## People in the Iranian Highlands

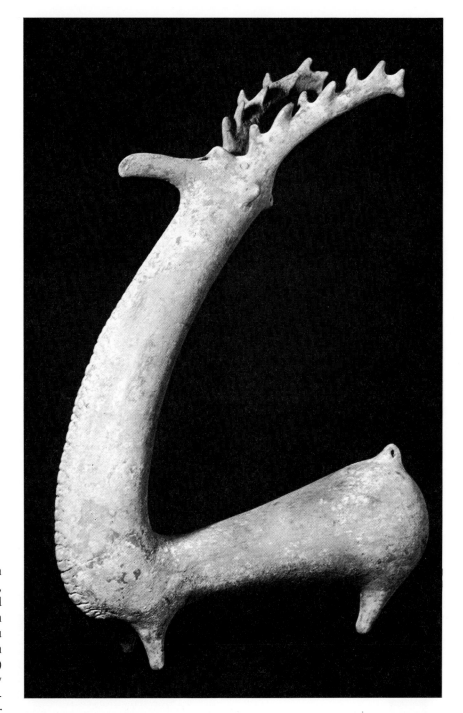

Terra-cotta *rhyton* (pouring vessel), from around the twelfth century BC, in the shape of a stag, that was perhaps found at Amlas

Several civilizations were already thriving in the ancient world when a hardy people, along with their horses and sheep, emerged from the grasslands of Central Asian Turkestan to settle on a great plateau between the Persian Gulf and the Caspian Sea. They called themselves Aryans (Irani) and their new homeland Irania. We know them as Persians because the Greek geographers made a mistake and named them after the province of Parsa. It was a long-lived error, since Persia did not officially become Iran until AD 1935. The Kurds, Bakhtiari, and Lurs are all descendants of these original Persian people, and still live in the western mountains.

As early as 4000 BC there was village life on the Iranian plateau. Iran was to become the heartland of the Persian Empire, which 2,500 years ago extended from the Indus Valley, in what is now Pakistan, to the Nile River and parts of present-day Libya.

Today the Islamic republic in southwestern Asia covers an area of over 635,932 square miles (over 1,647,063 square kilometers). It is bounded on the north by the former Soviet Union and the Caspian Sea, on the east by Pakistan and Afghanistan, on the south by the Persian Gulf and the Gulf of Oman, on the west by Iraq, and on the northwest by Turkey. More than 30 percent of its present-day boundary is seacoast. A series of massive mountain ranges surround Iran's high interior basin. Most of the country is above 1,500 feet (460 meters) high, and one-sixth of it is over four times that elevation. The mountainous areas are very rugged, almost unreachable, and populated mostly by pastoral nomads.

Iran's coastal regions outside her mountain ring are in sharp contrast to these elevations: the strip along the Caspian Sea in the north, frequently narrowing severely, falls from the high summits to the marshy lake's

edge below sea level. On the southern coast, the land falls away from a high plateau to meet the Persian and Oman Gulfs. This dry, barren, triangular-shaped plateau of Iran dominates most of the country, one-sixth of which consists of desert. Still, today, only about 10 percent of the land is arable, though agriculture manages to support roughly one-third of the population of over 61,000,000. According to popular belief, the huge unexplored salt waste in Iran's arid interior plateau contains the biblical city of Sodom.

In the course of the third and second millennium BC, the Indo-European people who settled on the mountain ridges that stretched east of Mesopotamia to the valley of the Indus River would play a significant role in world history as they gradually abandoned their nomadic lifestyle and settled down as farmers and cattle-herders. Among them were two groups, the Persians who stayed and the Indians who went on to the Asian subcontinent region between the Indus and the Ganges Rivers. The two cultures probably lived together around 2000 BC in the area that now makes up southern Russia and northern Iran. The earliest forms of their respective languages bear a strong resemblance to each other. Their religion and mythology contain many common elements.

Reference to this early contact is found in the *Avesta*, the sacred books of Zoroastrianism. The *Avesta* preserves the beliefs of their religion, Zoroastrianism, an ancient Persian religion reformed during the seventh and sixth centuries BC by a (some say legendary) prophet and religious teacher named Zoroaster, a name derived from the Greek form of a Persian name, Zarathushtra. He is said by those who consider him a historical figure to have lived seventy-seven years during a time of belief in many nature gods, and little is known about his existence beyond that. Zoroastrianism spread rapidly and, despite the onslaughts of Islam that began in the seventh century, it survives still. (About 80,000 Zoroastrians live today in parts of India, where they are known as Parsis, and in Pakistan. Another 18,000 live in Iran.)

The *Avesta* was compiled around AD 224, when Zoroastrianism became Iran's official religion, and is still the religion's scripture and prayer book. It describes the creation of a world peopled by Indo-Europeans, referring to a place called Airyana Vaeja. (Zoroaster converted Vishtaspa, king of Chorasmia, in a mountainous region by that name that is now northern Turkestan.)

Zoroaster rejected all but one of the many gods of his day. Ahura Mazda, or Ormazd, was the one he chose to be worshiped, while the personification of evil was named Ahriman. The world was created, he said, in the struggle between the two of them, and since then the battle between good and evil,

Bronze votive standard with demon and monsters, made in Luristan at the beginning of the first millennium BC

Bronze lion's head from Luristan. It was forged in the ninth century BC.

light and darkness, goes on. Zoroastrians later taught that history was a drama divided into four periods consisting of 3,000 years each, during which an equal number of major events take place. Each century thereafter will welcome its own prophet or savior as a successor to Zoroaster, it is said, until the final judgment and a new world.

The Zoroastrians have a hereditary priesthood, with a bishop heading important temples. Children are initiated at age seven to ten, when they receive a shirt and girdle that they wear throughout their lives. A sacred fire burns continually, and there are six annual festivals. A sacred liquor, bread, and milk are consumed during ceremonies.

Zoroastrianism was virtually obliterated under the dual impact of Greek conquest in the late fourth century BC and Islam in the seventh century AD. Most adherents who stayed were forced to become Muslim. Those who fled to India took the *Avesta* with them.

## The Sixteen Countries of the *Avesta*

According to those writings, the supreme god Ahura Mazda created sixteen countries. The first was Airyana Vaeja, the cradle of all (implicitly Indo-European) people. Although described as an area with many good features, it was given winter and serpents by the evil force, Angra Mainyu. Winter (considered by Ahura Mazda to be "the worst of all horrors") lasted for ten months, while summer lasted for two. This duality pervades the religion; for every good creation of Ahura Mazda, Angra Mainyu counters with a disaster. This feature recurs in various guises throughout Iranian religious history. It may have strongly influenced other religions, as well.

The second country was called Sogdiana. There Angra Mainyu created the locust that destroys crops and the resulting famine that destroys animals. The third country was Margiana between the Oxus River (Amu Darya) and the Caspian Sea. There Angra Mainyu created ants to counteract the blessings of Ahura Mazda. In the next place, Bactria, he created godlessness. The fifth country was Harokag, known as "the country where people leave the house," because relatives would leave the body of the deceased. This was in accordance with the wishes of Ahura Mazda. In response, Angra Mainyu created mourning and burial songs that belonged to the realm of evil forces.

Afterward, Ahura Mazda created Samarkand, Raga, Kabul, and Punjab, also known as India, or "the land of the seven rivers." For every new land, a new disaster or evil was created. These included a climate of excessive heat, pride, witchcraft, betrayal, and sodomy, and the crimes of disorder, sup-

Stone statuette of a fertility goddess that was made in the twentieth century BC and found at Tepe-Hissar

pression of the poor, and the practice of cremation or burial of the dead. (Parsis outside Bombay still build high platforms for their dead called "towers of silence." The corpses are picked clean by vultures rather than being cremated on funeral pyres in Hindu fashion, or buried. Passengers going in and out of the city by train can see the towers.)

After the stories about the different countries, the *Avesta* details a legend that is linked to the emigration of the Indians from Persia. Yima, the first Indo-European king of these tribal people, takes it upon himself "to extend the country." Ahura Mazda then asks him to act as a religious leader and lawgiver for his people. Yima refuses; he is only concerned with his tasks as a conqueror.

The *Avesta* describes three successive attempts by the Indo-Europeans at emigration, each led by Yima: "And next spoke I, Ahura Mazda, to the golden-curled Yima: O Yima, the country is full of herds, people, and dogs; there is no room for other people

363

inhabitants of the adjacent rich and powerful Mesopotamia on their western border. This change from nomadic lifestyle to agriculture has been attributed to Zoroaster, who wrote encouragement to his people: "I will act as tutor to those who want to cultivate a particular area."

Zoroaster glorifies the existence of the farmer, even writing him a lyrical hymn: "O, Creator of the world, thou holy god! In which place is the earth happier?"

Ahura Mazda answered: "In the place where the pious man fulfills his religious duties by singing hymns and by praying."

"O, Creator of the world, thou holy god! What is the second happiest place on earth?"

Ahura Mazda answered: "It is the place where there is a house with a priest and cattle and a wife and children; and where the cattle breeds and the wife works and the child grows up; where the fire burns and life develops."

"O, Creator of the world, thou holy god! What is the third happiest place on earth?"

Ahura Mazda answered: "It is the place where the farmer sows wheat or harvests hay and fruit; where the farmer waters what is dry and dries what is wet."

"O, Creator of the world! What is the fourth happiest place on earth?"

Ahura Mazda answered: "It is the place where one herds and drives the cattle."

"O, Creator of the world! What is the fifth happiest place on earth?"

Ahura Mazda answered: "It is the place where the herds bear so much manure that one can get warm from the glow of it."

The sequence indicates a preference for agriculture over cattle-breeding and the nomadic way of lifestyle. The great changes in the life of the Persians also left their mark on religion. As they traded the inhospitable steppes of Asia for the warm and fertile area of Iran, the Persians came to believe that certain parts of the steppes belonged to evil spirits.

This horse's head from the seventh century BC once probably formed part of a column.

Bronze bit from a horse's harness with mountain goats from Luristan. It was made in the eighth century BC.

Relief found in the ruins of the Citadel of Persepolis. The king is sitting on his throne receiving a subject.

# Zarathushtra

## Religion and the Romans

The Persian name of the prophet the Greeks called Zoroaster was Spitama (his family name) Zarathushtra (his given name). He was born about 630 BC or earlier in Airyana Vaeja, a mountainous region of eastern Persia where people regarded cattle as sacred. The young prophet took this belief into his own new theology.

Nothing about Zarathushtra or his dates is securely documented. Many legends about his youth might offer insight into his personality, but it is difficult to determine whether they have any foundation in fact. Apparently as a young man he had visions of the god he called Ahura Mazda (the "Lord Wisdom"). (The conversations he had with that benevolent spirit are written in metric form in *Psalms in the Gathas*, part of the Zoroastrian

Tomb of the
Persian king Cyrus
the Great
in Pasargadae

Metal jar handle
shaped like a winged goat.
It dates from the time
of the Achaemenid kings
(fifth century BC).

scripture called the *Avesta*.) During a period of great drought, Zarathushtra was said to have distributed his father's stores of food to the poor. On another occasion, he tried to save a half-starved dog and its five pups. When he was twenty, he left his parents' house on a search for the most just and most merciful person he could find. For seven years, his parents heard nothing from him. Fragments from his time of meditations in a cave are recorded in the *Zend-Avesta*.

Zarathushtra searched for a reconciliation between the established cults that adhered to old magic beliefs and the truth as he saw it. He accepted the view of the cult of fire, which held that sacred flames make everything impure disappear into smoke.

The prophet struggled for many years to convince people of the purity of his new faith. He found little basis for his thinking in the previous work of others, and was evidently not particularly eloquent himself. Nevertheless, like Muhammad ten centuries later, Zarathushtra considered himself the person to free his people from the grip of irrational superstition. He may have been initially educated as a magician or shaman. "As a priest," he said, "I will continue to search for the paths of righteousness and teach the way to cultivate the earth."

Zarathushtra was apparently subject to some persecution. He writes: "To which country shall I flee? Where shall I hide? My friends and the nobles desert me and neither the people nor the liars who rule the earth will take me in. How can I ever satisfy you, Ahura Mazda? Now I see that I have failed. I have few friends in my house and few cattle in my stables. Do not desert me, Ahura Mazda. Help me as a friend who helps his friends. Teach me to think well and correctly."

## Successful Prophet

Evidently Zarathushtra's prayers were answered. After ten years of preaching, he made his first convert: his cousin Maidiomana became a disciple. Two years

later, a local king, Hystaspes, was converted and devoted himself zealously to the new religion. The king and the prophet became close friends. Zarathushtra had earlier tried to gain followers among the nomad tribes of south-central Asia. He had failed there, as he had in his own country. A precursor of Constantine the Great, Hystaspes undertook conquests to impose Zarathushtra's teachings on the neighboring people. He convert-

ed his entire court to the new religion. The king's brother, his sons, Queen Atosa, the vizier Zarathrustra, and his brother Yamaspes are all named in the *Avesta* as members of the circle of disciples that surrounded the prophet. Some songs of praise from the sacred book are attributed to them.

The prophet often addresses them directly: "And I speak at this meeting of holy men the just words of Ahura Mazda and sing the praises of the good spirit. I speak the truth which I see rise from the flames of this fire. Embrace the spirit of the earth, plow the

Detail of a relief in Darius's audience hall in Persepolis showing subjects of the Persian king paying him tribute

Persian king fights a lion monster. Relief from Darius's palace at Persepolis.

Ruins of the royal palace of Persepolis, the city that Darius built as capital of his kingdom

Griffin that originally formed the top of a column in the palace of Persepolis

fields, watch the flames of the holy fire. Everyone, man or woman, must choose between good and evil. You, descendants of noble ancestors, approve of my message, arise!"

It is not known exactly where King Hystaspes's court was located. He was probably not a major king but a local ruler who had to pay tribute to the neighboring nomadic Tartars. Urged on by the new belief and the prophet, Hystaspes waged two holy wars against the Tartars and ended this humiliating situation. That success abroad greatly enhanced the reputation of the new faith among the Persian and Indo-European people. The wars (which might have been limited to repelling Tartar raiders trying to collect tribute) were apparently waged during the final years of Zarathushtra's life.

It is believed that the prophet was murdered in 550 BC by fanatic Tartars or a hostile magician, defending his old faith. In some legends, Zarathushtra's death is depicted as a supernatural event. He is said to have been carried off to heaven by a flash of lightning to save him from cruel tortures.

After his death, the old superstitions seemed to gain ground while Zarathushtra's fame grew. The prophet was probably deified quite soon after he died. The *Avesta* contains prayers addressed to him: "To Mazda and Zarathushtra whom we revere, this prayer is directed." He was depicted with wings and a royal scepter. He was also later identified with the magicians who were his worst enemies.

### The Role of the Magi

Most priests (called Magi) belonged to the Median tribe, which often rivaled the Persians and required tribute of them. The Magi adapted Zarathushtra's teachings and used the prophet's broad influence for their own gain. In the *Avesta*, fragments of Zarathushtra's original teachings are found mingled with age-old texts about the evil spirits of the steppe area and detailed descriptions of magicians' rites.

Descriptions on how to purify a person who has touched a dead body or a dead dog cover many pages. Even the cut hair and clipped nails of the living were considered dead parts of the body, contaminated and to be avoided. The one who cuts hair or nails must stand at least ten steps away from other people, twenty steps away from the fire, thirty steps from water, all to prevent contamination. According to some scholars, Zarathushtra wrote much more in the *Avesta* than what has survived. Twelve thousand parchment cowhides of his writings are believed to have been destroyed in the great fire of Persepolis, the Persian capital, c.331 BC.

### The Struggle between Good and Evil

Zarathushtra preached worship of a benevolent Ahura Mazda and spoke of the dualism existing between good and evil. The good spirit, Spenta Mainyu, a manifestation of Ahura Mazda, is said to battle its opposite spirit, Angra Mainyu, who has chosen evil. The first spirit works toward unity and building; the second only tries to destroy. Humans must choose between the two. If they opt for the side of good, the positive, they support Ahura Mazda in his work. The good spirit can only triumph when people assist in building and uniting. Ahura Mazda demands right thinking, truth, power, devotion, health, and life (all manifestations of good) from his followers. The prophet Zarathushtra's overall perspective is benign, since he drew from his early acceptance of the cult of fire that evil on earth would ultimately be purified by fire and molten metal.

### The *Avesta*

Zarathushtra seemed to attempt to meld the religious notions of his time. The *Gathas*, which are believed to have been written by the prophet himself, take a monotheistic approach. *The Liturgy of the Seven Chapters*, written after his death in a similar dialect, praises his teaching but draws on a range of cult beliefs that ignore Angra Mainyu, quite unlike the first section. The cult of fire, important in the religious life of the Persians, probably added the concept of water as holy about this time. Water was personified in the goddess Anahitis. She was considered subservient to the god of fire; water can only cleanse, while fire can destroy all impurity. In Zarathushtra's lifetime, Ahura Mazda, seen as the god of fire, still reigned by himself. In *Seven Chapters*, Ahura Mazda acts like the Aryan god Varuna described in the ancient scripture, the *Rig-Veda*. Both have wives associated with water: Ahuranis with Ahura and Varunanis with Varuna. Both are guardians of truth and watch over the world through the eye of the sun.

The *Gathas* and the *Seven Chapters* are incorporated in a liturgy known as the *Yasna*. It combines aspects of Aryan polytheism with Zoroastrianism in ceremonies

Gate of King Xerxes
in the Citadel of Persepolis,
guarded by winged beasts
with human heads

The Persian Empire

Original Persian Territory
Conquest during Rule
of Cyprus
Conquest during Rules
of Cambyses and Darius
Cyprus Great Campaigns

371

A group of decorated columns in the ruins of the royal audience hall in Persepolis

consisting mainly of hymns (called *Yashts*) to a variety of deities.

The last section of the *Avesta* (called the *Vendidad*) was written in the fourth century BC, and deals primarily with rituals and law. The Greeks who had conquered Persia by then found a religion far more magical in orientation that the original conception of Zarathushtra. The Greek historian Herodotus considered many of the Persian rituals to be of Magi origin, including those advocating the protection of dogs and the funeral practice of leaving corpses to the elements rather than burying or cremating them.

**Persian Lifestyle**
The effect of the Persians' religious practice on their lifestyle is what Herodotus describes here, though he may also be incorporating aspects of early Iranian religion.

"The Persians have neither statues of gods, nor temples, nor altars [Note: art and archaeological evidence says otherwise.] They also bring offerings to the god of the sun, the moon, fire, water, and wind. Of all feasts, the most important one for the Persians is their birthday. After personal courage, they most admire fertility: each year the king sends gifts to the family with the most children. Children are taught only three things between the ages of five and twenty: horseback riding, archery, and telling the truth. The most contemptuous deed is to tell a lie and after that comes going into debt. The Persians never pollute the water of their rivers with garbage, and neither do they wash their hands in them. They consider the rivers to be holy."

The Persians led a harsh existence in the highlands of Iran. "Before they set out to conquer the world," as Herodotus writes, "they owned almost nothing before the conquest of Sardis." It is said that in the sixth century BC, when Croesus of Lydia (in Asia Minor) prepared for war with the Persians, one of his counselors advised him: "You are going to war against people who wear leather pants, live off dry ground, drink water rather than wine, and do not know figs. If you conquer them, you will still own nothing. If they vanquish you they will be incredibly rich."

Whatever their reputation, the Persian lifestyle certainly did not exclude a love of

Gold coin of Cyrus the Younger (424–401 BC). He was a son of Darius II and the brother of Artaxerxes II. The latter tried to depose him, but did not succeed.

Relief found in Persepolis, portraying a member of the royal bodyguard

373

Relief on the upper
half of the grave of Darius II,
depicting the king
worshiping at Naqsh-I
Rustam

wine; the alcoholic tendencies of Cambyses, Cyrus's son, was legendary. Herodotus reports: "It is their custom to discuss business when they are drunk, but they only make their decisions the next day, when they are sober again."

Zarathushtra (in contrast to Muhammad) did not ban the use of alcohol. It was customary among the Indo-European tribes to imbibe an intoxicating drink called *haoma*. The Vedic word for what was probably the same drink was *soma*. It appears to have been widely used in the ceremonies of the Persian shamans and magicians.

## The Medes

Among the Indo-European tribes appearing in the second millennium BC in the Persian highlands were the Medes, a loose gathering of tribes. Their capital was in Ekbatana (present-day Hamadan in central western Iran). They were allied with the Babylonians in the destruction of Nineveh in 612 BC. Nineveh was so thoroughly destroyed that it was never rebuilt, ending Assyrian control. In the early part of the sixth century, the Persians won the leadership of the tribes when Cyrus won over the allegiance of the Median army, who handed their king over to him, and important changes began to appear.

## Cyrus the Great (Cyrus II)

The small mountain kingdom of the Persians became the nucleus of a mighty empire. Under the leadership of the ambitious Cyrus the Great (559–530 BC), it defeated the Medes in around 550, Lydia in 547, and the Babylonians in 539.

Cyrus was probably not a true Persian. Herodotus says that he was the son of a Median princess and a Persian king (Cambyses I). Cyrus, not a follower of Zarathushtra, appeared to embody the broad religious tolerance practiced at the time. Persians often identified the gods of the people they conquered with benevolent spirits already familiar to them. In Babylon, Cyrus gave the exiled Jews permission to return to

Gold plaque from
the Oxus treasure. It depicts
a Persian soldier
or priest.

375

Relief from the northern staircase of the reception hall in the Citadel of Persepolis. It depicts a lion attacking a bull.

their country and rebuild their temple. He returned the statues of gods to tribes deported by the Assyrians. When he arrived in Babylon, he was humble, but kingly, respectful of the ancient culture. He had the temples and sacrifices to the gods restored.

Cyrus made his capital at Pasargadae, in the southern part of Iran. Remnants of palaces and pavilions of his time have been found there. A relief on a gate shows a winged guardian figure wearing a tall crown. The empty tomb of Cyrus has been located on the plain of Murghab.

## Cambyses II (529–522 BC)

Cyrus's son, Cambyses II, inherited the empire. A few hieroglyphic texts in Egypt and Herodotus refer to him. After Cyrus II was mortally wounded in a battle against nomadic tribes of central Asia in 529, his son Cambyses II ascended the throne. Under his direction, the Persians conquered Egypt in 525 and added it to the empire. Despite the horror stories of Herodotus, who visited Egypt himself in the mid-fifth century BC, Cambyses appears to have followed his father's policy of religious tolerance. Like his father, he was not really interested in the teachings of Zarathushtra. He had the

Top of a Persian column decorated with the heads of two joined bulls, from the palace of Artaxerxes II in Susa

376

Glazed brick wall from the palace in Susa decorated with the image of two winged lions with human heads

Egyptian temples restored and participated in their ceremonies as a pharaoh would.

## Darius I (522–486 BC)

After the death of Cambyses II in 522 BC, the Magi (Median priests) sought to gain power. They were defeated in 522 by an insurrection of Persian nobles under the leadership of the Persian Darius. The insur- rection destroyed the power of the Medes and other rebels. Darius, a follower of Zarathushtra, took over. His inscriptions present him as a worshiper of Ahura Mazda who regards a lie as an evil force in the world. Many recovered texts associated with Darius seem directly taken from the *Avesta*. For example, Darius's statement inscribed on the Behistun rock:

"Thus said Darius, the great king: These people (the Magians) rose up; lies had made them rebellious and they themselves misled the people. Ahura Mazda delivered them into my hands. All that I have done, I have done thanks to Ahura Mazda. You who read this: believe me, for there are no lies here. May Ahura Mazda be witness to the truth in this story about my many important exploits."

Darius expanded the empire, establishing an administration completely different in nature from the oppressive reign of the Assyrians. Slavery was unknown. Under Darius, the Persians developed their own art

Detail of a glazed brick frieze depicting a Persian guard. It was found in Artaxerxes's palace in Susa.

forms. They did not develop their own writing system, however, but adopted the Mesopotamian cuneiform.

### Persian Rule

Darius's son and successor, Xerxes I (reigning from 486–465), who unsuccessfully invaded Greece in 480 BC, also worshiped Ahura Mazda. There is evidence that he believed Arta (Truth) would be attained after death. This reflects the Aryan notion of Rta (also Truth).

Artaxerxes I (son of Xerxes I, reigning from 464 to 425 BC) likewise worshiped Ahura Mazda. The Magian influence on the teachings of Zarathushtra was probably first manifested about this time.

Under Artaxerxes II (son of Darius II, reigning from 404 to 359 BC), this polytheistic blending continued as the first Persian temples were built.

Persians worshiped a variety of deities for centuries (especially under the Greek Seleucids, from 312 to 64 BC, and Parthian Arsacids, from about 250 BC to AD 266. Only under Persian rule again, with the advent of the Sassanid dynasty (AD 226–641), was Zoroastrianism made the official religion. It was forced to give way to Islam with the Arab conquest of Persia in the seventh century.

The Persians recognized the right of the conquered peoples to continue living in their own way as independently as possible. It was this remarkable tolerance which enabled the Persians to split their enormous empire into twenty *satrapies* or autonomous areas. Persian rule was a mixed blessing for a large number of regions. It encountered little resistance, even in Ionia, on the west coast of Asia Minor, which was completely Greek.

Two parties came into being in the western satrapies. One party comprised aristocrats, the members of the senate who were primarily rich financiers and wealthy landowners. The other was a people's party. It relied on the city councils and was often led by a leader of the people or *tyrant* (a chief official elected by direct vote of the people). The peoples' party controlled the large cities of Ionia, Miletus, Smyrna, Phocea, and the islands of Naxos and Samos. The Persian satraps worked both with the aristocrats and the people's parties. Next to the *satrap* (usually a member of the Persian royal family) stood the chancellor, who was leader of the army and the police. Special representatives from each satrapy made periodic reports to keep the king informed.

The Persian king resided in the capital city of Susa, as well as in Babylon and Persepolis. Taxes were levied at the same rate throughout the empire: 10 percent of all profits. That was exceptionally low, considering that taxes in Egypt were 33 percent and in Babylon 20 percent of profits. The regular collecting of these taxes allowed the satraps to send large sums of money to the capital. The Persian kings amassed great wealth. Alexander the Great found a treasury with 550 tons (500,000 kilograms) of silver in the Susa palace.

The tax money was spent on the army, the administration, and public works, including the renowned Persian roads. The central highway, known as the Royal Road, led from Susa near the Persian Gulf to Sardis in Asia Minor, a distance of 1,500 miles (2,414 kilometers).

Statue of Shiva, the god of destruction, with his wife, Parvati

# Indo-Europeans in India

## The Route to the Indus Valley

Waves of pastoral Indo-Aryans from somewhere near the Caspian Sea traversed the western foothills of the Himalayas around 1500 BC. They were part of the great Indo-European migrations to the Indus Valley in India that had begun a few hundred years earlier. The tribal name *Arya*, notoriously misused as *Aryan* by the Nazis of the twentieth century to describe Caucasians of non-Jewish descent, has no validity as an ethnic term.

The route that the Indo-Aryans followed probably led along the Khyber Pass. Even today this ravine between cliffs and mountains is dangerous and virtually impassable. Overhanging cliffs threaten the traveler for 45 miles (77 kilometers) along a desert landscape, while on the other side lies the luxuriant vegetation of the Indus Valley.

The oldest religion known today began there, evolving by itself with no individual founder and no established doctrine. The name *Hindu* comes from the Sanskrit word *Sindhu* or *Indus*, meaning river or great water. Over 500 million people practice Hinduism today, primarily on the Indian subcontinent and its adjacent lands, but also on the Pacific Islands in Southeast Asia, in Africa, and in the Americas.

### The Old Indian Civilization

Upon their arrival the Indo-Aryans encoun-

Panorama in northeast modern Afghanistan. This is the Khyber Pass, a route to India that some Indo-Aryans may have used.

tered other tribes, native peoples of the Indus Valley who lived in fortified cities and had formed a confederation in order to resist invaders.

During excavations in the Indus Valley at the beginning of this century, two native cities were discovered that defy the designation "primitive." The two cities, called Harappa and Mohenjo-Daro ("the mound of the dead"), were built about 2500 BC. They covered a considerable area. Mohenjo-Daro is three-quarters of a mile (1.2 kilometers) long and one-third of a mile (.53 kilometer) wide. The streets are broad and straight, running north and south or east and west. Lined with two- and three-room dwellings, they follow one another without interruption. The

houses, some of which had two or more stories, were built of brick. Many houses were provided with toilets. There was a sewage system with earthenware pipes that kept the city clean. Monumental constructions include huge fortifying walls that have lasted 4,000 years and an immense brick-lined tank now called the Great Bath, which may originally have had a ritual function.

Everything indicates that Harappa and Mohenjo-Daro were built according to a predetermined plan. There may be many more such ancient cities lying buried beneath the sand of the Indus Valley.

There has been much discussion concerning the events and factors leading to the end of the Indus civilization. One opinion holds that a variety of natural factors, such as a decline in rainfall and increase in population, were responsible. Other positions seek to find an explanation in calamitous natural events, such as a sudden change in the course of the Indus River and the drying up of the Sarasvati-Ghaggar River. A third list of possible causes involves the invasive actions of humans, such as the movement of groups of tribesmen into the Indus Valley from the hills to the west, or the arrival of Indo-Aryans. Also it is thought that the breakdown of trade contacts with Mesopotamia during the opening centuries of the second millennium may have contributed to the weakening of the Indus cities. A fourth group of hypothetical causes includes the possibility of epidemics, which would explain the presence in the streets of the bodies that were later discovered by archaeologists.

From the material remains that have been unearthed, it has been deduced that the Indus Valley was densely populated at this time and that contact might have long existed between the Indus Valley and ancient Mesopotamia. However, it remains unclear who exactly the Indus Valley inhabitants were, whether they formed a single tribe, and how they organized their social system. The Indo-Aryans saw them, to quote the *Rig-Veda*, as "wild folk who had been cast out by Brahman [Lord]: They eat meat, and their presence is distasteful." They are described as "noseless," "people without laws," and "people with a black skin."

The attitude that the newcomers adopted toward the native population would seem to indicate that they found themselves overwhelmed. They had to contend with a vast population in a vast area. Separation and segregation seemed to offer the Indo-Aryans a means of preserving their own identity and maintaining authority. The result was the caste system.

## The Caste System

The caste system, probably instituted by the Indo-Aryans after their arrival in India, created extensive segregation within Indian society. The term *caste*, which is one used by Europeans, is from the Portuguese *casta* (breed). An Indian term for the same social structure is *jati* (birth). The *Vedas* distinguish *varnas* (colors) of people in Indian society as a way to distinguish the lighter-skinned Indo-Aryan conquerors from the darker Dravidians, though with a few exceptions castes are not physically distinguishable from each other. The word came to indicate social divisions based on occupation.

Each caste is subject to a great number of strict *tabus* (prohibitions) that regulate marriage, burial, and daily life. In ancient times there were only four castes: the *Brahmans* or priests, the *Kshatriyas* or warriors, the *Vaisyas* or tradespeople and landowners, and the *Shudras* or servants. Ultimately, some 3,000 castes evolved.

The warriors commanded the greatest respect among the Indo-Aryans. The social prominence of the Brahmans (or temple priests) dates from a later period. The earliest *rishis* (sages or wise men) were often financially dependent on the noble families.

When the Indo-Aryans first came to India they were divided into three social classes: the warriors or aristocracy, the priests, and the common people. There was no consciousness of caste; professions were not hereditary, nor were there rules limiting marriage within classes or taboos about the sharing of food. The first step in the direction of a caste system was taken when the Indo-Aryans looked on the indigenous people as

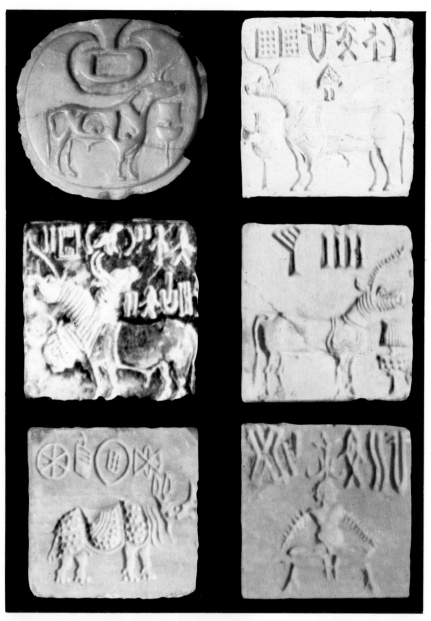

Seals made of steatite bearing images of various animals, dating from the time before the Indo-Aryans entered the region of the Indus

A large tank called the Great Bath, found in ancient Mohenjo-Daro, a city built in the Indus Valley around 2500 BC

381

View of the excavations of the ancient city of Harappa

lower than they, probably a result of their fear of these peoples, and the even greater fear that assimilation with them would lead to a loss of Indo-Aryan identity. The establishment of caste was no doubt promoted by other factors as well, including the fact that, with the transition from nomadic pastoralism to a settled agrarian economy, specialization of labor gradually became a marked feature of Indo-Aryan society and a natural breeding ground for such a hierarchical system.

The Indo-Aryan invasion forced many inhabitants to flee to the hills and forests. Little by little they resettled on the outskirts of the villages and began to perform various kinds of work. The Indo-Aryans used these "inferiors" to trade their products, to manufacture tools and ornaments, to herd their flocks, to work their land, and to remove the human and animal waste from their settlements. Each of these occupations became a caste.

One of the seals found
in Mohenjo-Daro depicting
a horned animal and
the Indus script, undeciphered
to this day

This system had very strict rules. Violation of the rules was thought to lead to ritual impurity. Contact with a member of a lower caste was said to defile a person. Some people were said to defile others merely by casting a shadow on them or by overstepping a specified distance between them. There were complicated rules for purifying oneself.

The distances between the various castes had a tendency to increase over the course of time. The Shudras or servants, in particular, became increasingly isolated. Other castes avoided them, as contact with them caused such impurity. They were also excluded from religious ceremonies. No Brahman was permitted to accept a drink of water from a Shudra, but he could accept a gift. The *Atharva-Veda* recommended that a Brahman receiving a gift from a Shudra accept it in silence. On the other hand, he was to accept a gift from another Brahman with holy words, a gift from a Kshatriya with thanks spoken aloud, and a gift from a Vaisya with thanks murmured under his breath.

One of the most important indicators of the social hierarchy was manifested in the rules governing the giving and taking of food. Within these rules, one could not accept food cooked by a person ritually lower than oneself, as the food would be considered unclean. However, one could accept food offered by a person ritually higher than oneself.

Head of a man, made of steatite and found in the ruins of Mohenjo-Daro

Statue of the god Vishnu in his incarnation as a wild boar. He is one of the most important gods of Hinduism.

383

## The Untouchables

Below the rungs of the caste ladder, outside the system of recognized people, are millions of people, outcastes called the Untouchables. Traditionally ignored, they were regarded as unclean, like the work they typically performed. They cleaned the latrines and skinned the carcasses used for meat and leather. They were not even allowed to walk where the caste Hindus did, or to use the same wells or temples. In the twentieth century, the incomparable Indian leader Mahatma Gandhi called them the "Children of God" and personally underscored his message by taking on the humble tasks traditionally assigned to this caste.

## Modern India

Despite the fact that the caste system was officially abolished, through the efforts of Gandhi, by the first government of independent India under Jawaharlal Nehru, it still exists as a social phenomenon. What existed, and still does, is a great difference in the opportunities available to the lower castes. The Indian government instituted a means of affirmative action based on the recognition that there is, in fact, no difference between the people of the various castes. There are places reserved for various castes at the universities and in government service. People of all caste levels are evident today in all professions.

## The *Vedas*

The *Vedas* (from the Sanskrit word *Veda* for knowledge) are the four sacred texts of Hinduism. Also called the *Samhitas* (collection), the books are the *Rig-Veda* (the oldest work), the *Sama-Veda*, the *Yajur-Veda*, and the *Atharva-Veda*. All are collections of hymns, poetry, and proscribed rituals that were originally part of an oral tradition transmitted and elaborated on by rishis for generations before they were written down in Vedic, or early Sanskrit. The oldest parts of them date from 1300 to 1000 BC and are apparently of Indo-Aryan origin. Their present form dates from the end of the third century BC.

## The *Rig-Veda*

The *Rig-Veda* is a collection of more than a thousand hymns (*rig* in Sanskrit), compiled around 3200 BC and set in ten books. The Indo-Aryans are credited with its authorship, making it the oldest of the Hindu sacred writings. The verses, believed to have originated orally, reflect the delight of the immigrants in their new land. The warmth of the sunlight and the Indus River itself made a deep impression on them: "We have crossed over the other side of darkness. O, Dawn, you have prepared the way, you shine and smile like the rhythm of a poem and your lovely face has made us joyful. . . . The sun goddess wakes the sleeping men to go forth. One goes to amuse himself; another goes to the assembly, deeply interested in the things that he encounters. The Dawn has awakened all living beings. . . . Shimmering, sparkling, the Indus, the river richest in floods, brings its water to the surface like an untamed wild stallion."

Indra was one of the most important Vedic gods. He is the protector of war and is here seated on a three-headed elephant.

384

### The *Sama-Veda*

The *Sama-Veda* verses are hymns or songs primarily adopted from the *Rig-Veda* and used by the *udgatri* (chanters), special priests who conducted certain rituals.

### The *Yajur-Veda*

The *Yajur-Veda* uses similar material but adds an emphasis on sacrifice. Its priests chanted the requisite accompaniment to the sacrifices they performed.

### The *Atharva-Veda*

The *Atharva-Veda* is controversial and full of magical incantations. Of later origin than the other books, it was finally adopted because of its accepted use as a manual of ritual by the Brahmans, the highest ranking priests.

### Supplementary Writings

The poetic sections of each *Veda*, regarded by scholars as the oldest, are called the *mantras*. Prose commentaries, called the *Brahmanas*, that explain liturgical or religious details are appended to the *Vedas*. These are further explained by the

Statue of the goddess Kali, a fierce aspect of Shiva's wife. Kali is the goddess of destruction and death, and her worshipers made human sacrifices in her honor.

# Relations between East and West

In the ancient world, cultural exchanges often occurred between East and West. Achaemenid Persians linked the two regions in the sixth century BC, making the northwestern region of the Indian subcontinent a satrapy of their empire. The army that Xerxes led against Greece in the fifth century BC included detachments of Indians.

Greeks extended their sphere of influence to the East through the conquests of Alexander the Great, beginning in 334 BC. Before his death in 323, he had established an extraordinary empire, initiating his invasion of India in 327 by overthrowing a number of Persian satrapies in the northwest. As a result of the divisiveness among the small principalities in that region, he had no difficulty in conquering them as well. His campaign lasted only about two years and left few traces, as the Greek troops left quickly. None of the contemporary Indian sources of the time mention this expedition.

Its most important result was to establish Greek governors in the region of northwest India. This Greek population contributed greatly to the rise of trade between India and the West. The conquerors had departed so quickly, they left a power vacuum promptly filled by Chandra Gupta Maurya, one of a great number of local kings. He set up his realm in the Punjab at the expense of the Seleucids, who controlled the eastern portion of Alexander's conquests. After the two powers concluded a military treaty, a small but intensive cultural exchange began.

Toward the middle of the third century BC, India reached its high point during the reign of King Asoka. Contacts with the West were considerably extended. Classical civilization met its eastern counterpart. Western and eastern elements existed side by side, mutually influencing one another in the field of national and city government, culture, and

religion. In the West, this was a time of transition from the independent Greek city-state to the centralized Roman world empire.

As the power of the Romans increased, trade between India and the West expanded. A great stream of merchandise was sent along the trade routes from Asia to the West. The luxuries of India–perfume, precious stones, pearls, pepper, cinnamon, sugarcane, and cotton–were particularly prized in the Mediterranean area.

Trade routes always result in an exchange of culture, religion, and ideas. This statue in a chapel of a Buddhist monastery in Afghanistan has the features of Hercules, the Greco-Roman hero.

gious details are appended to the *Vedas*. These are further explained by the *Aranyakas* ("forest treatises") composed by Brahmans writing in wilderness seclusion. These conclude with the *Upanishads*, from the word for "sitting down near a teacher." This is a reference to the time when the *gurus* (wise men) began to gather students around them to share their wisdom, rather than meditating in isolation. The *Upanishads* are philosophical works that use allegory and moral insight as a means of teaching ethical concepts.

< The famous bronze statue of Shiva Nataraja, or "Dancing Shiva," considered by some to be the supreme god of Hinduism

A temple in Khajuraho. ❯
The outside of the building is
covered in reliefs depicting gods
and important events.

## The Hindu Gods

Despite the fact that it had no single founder and has no central doctrine, there is a central concept of god in Hinduism: Brahman, the God within and above all others (and there are many of them). All other gods are considered but aspects of the One.

Below and yet part of the all-pervasive Brahman, topping the pantheon of other deities, are Brahma the creator, Vishnu the preserver of life, and Shiva the destroyer. Shiva and Vishnu, like the other gods, are widely depicted in hundreds of forms, all part of the immensely rich world of Indian art, literature, music, and drama. Shiva can create life as well as end it and is venerated throughout India via the *lingam*, a pillar representing, among other things, the creative potentiality of life. Villagers bring flowers, rice, and fruit as symbolic offerings to the lingam in the local temples. Shiva is often worshiped as the god Nataraja, who carries the fire of destruction and the drum, a symbol for time. His consort, Parvati, goddess of the mountains, carries within herself the creative ability of woman, called *shakti*. Parvati, in her active role, is often called Shakti. Ultimately, all the female goddesses are aspects of the great goddess Devi.

Vishnu comes to earth in the forms of ten *avatars* (descents). These include the actual historical person of Buddha and the mythical heroes Krishna and Rama, subjects of the great epics the *Mahabharata* and the *Ramayana*.

Thirty-three gods are mentioned in the *Rig-Veda*, or three families of eleven gods each. Most are only vaguely described or are attributes of other gods. Many of these gods come from an ancient tradition and are comparable to gods from Greek, Roman, or Persian mythology. Among them are *Dyaus Pitar* (analogous to Zeus Pater of the Romans); *Usas* or the Dawn (the Roman Aurora); *Indra*, the god of storms and wars and a great lover of the alcoholic drink *soma*; and *Varuna* (the Roman Uranus or the Zoroastrian Ahura Mazda), ultimate authority over the gods.

Agni, the god of fire,
riding a cow. Agni is sometimes
depicted with two heads. One head
symbolizes the fire in
the hearth of a house, the other
symbolizes sacrificial fire.

389

## The Hindu Stages of Life

It is said of a certain King Ganaka that he summoned learned people to his court to study philosophical questions. The discussions concerned issues of general human interest: How is it possible that people can be freed from death by bringing sacrifices? If death swallows everything, who swallows death? What is the purpose of humankind? What is the power that rules everything, and yet is different from everything else? There were no definite answers, but in one allegory King Ganaka saw his capital in flames and said, "My city and my palace are burning, but, fortunately, nothing of myself."

This emphasis on the unimportance of possessions and objects and reverence for the inner life is part of Hinduism. Yet the *Vedas* also posit the ideal house of a Hindu as a gathering place for many, including beggars and poor people, servants, and protégés. Such a home is an intricate organism that feeds itself and is almost completely independent, from an economic point of view. According to the *Vedas*, which reflect the patriarchal subjection of women common at the time of their writing, the ideal wife is responsible for protecting the purity of her husband. She must prepare his meals and must keep impure food out of the house. She takes ritual baths to cleanse and ornament her body, so that her beauty will shine within her husband's home. She must say her prayers daily, but always separately from her husband. Thus pampered, the ideal husband has only to concern himself with poetry or art, surrounded by friends and relatives from his own caste.

The *Vedas* teach that a normal life can be harmonious if lived in four stages (*ashramas*, or refuges), with an acceptance of the obligations of each step. The student stage (*brahmacharin*) is first, with young people studying right living and service under a teacher, the guru. (This is often interpreted to mean the student's obligation to take his academic studies very seriously.) The second stage comes with marriage, family, and community responsibilities (*grihasta*). The third stage (*vanaprastha*) leads to a detachment from those duties and the material concerns inherent in them, and a concentration on retreat into the forest. The final stage (*sunnyasin*) is preparation for the next life, in which the seeker becomes a homeless wanderer without worldly attachments.

Present life is seen as only one journey of many taken by the essential aspect or soul (*atman*) of each individual. The idea of reincarnation is basic to Hinduism. All living things are involved in an endless cycle of birth and rebirth and much depends on *karma* (action), the law of cause and effect. This rests on a belief in spiritual ascent: If life is lived correctly, in accordance with the way of *dharma* (which implies an acceptance of one's station in life, one's caste), one can return in the next life at a higher level. Even plants and animals are considered subject to this. They can return as humans, or vice versa. (A greedy person can come back as a crow, one of the millions all over India that pick insatiably at anything resembling food.)

The ultimate goal is union with *Brahman*, the supreme being, the source of life itself. Only then is one liberated from the cycles of worldly existence, *moksha*.

This terra-cotta statuette found in the Indus Valley probably depicts a fertility goddess.

Chains made of steatite and carnelian beads found in the Indus Valley

A group of *moai*, statues on Easter Island. On this island 260 statues have been found, their height varying from 13 to 98 feet (4 to 30 meters).

# Cultures of the Pacific

*Australia, Indonesia, Melanesia, Micronesia, and Polynesia*

In the vast spaces between the coasts of Asia and America are scattered islands and *archipelagoes* (groups of islands) that seem to serve as stepping-stones from one continent to the other. These islands were once inhabited by the descendants of daring seafaring people who moved from island to island over a great part of the Pacific. Early explorers called the Pacific Ocean the South Sea, and throughout history we hear of the South Sea Islands, also known as Oceania, which consist of 25,000 islands, together with

Australia and New Zealand. Only a relative few of these islands are inhabited; some are no more than coral *atolls* (reefs surrounding lagoons).

The great migration in the Pacific area occurred by fits and starts. From 30,000 to 25,000 years ago, various peoples came to settle in New Guinea and Australia by way of the Indonesian archipelago. They reached Tasmania in about 9000 BC. Much later, between 2500 and 1500 BC, a second migration took place. The Micronesians arrived,

391

View of the island of Bora-Bora on an engraving from Louis-Isidore Duperrey's book *A Voyage around the World*

Painted wooden paddle
from Polynesia

driven from Indonesia by other migrating peoples. They left traces as far as Polynesia. Their only permanent settlements, however, were in Micronesia. In all other areas, they were driven out or exterminated by later waves of immigrants. It is assumed that the migrants of AD 100 to 1000 followed two routes: a northern path through the Caroline and the Marshall Islands, and a southern one, through New Guinea and Samoa to the central archipelagoes of the Pacific. From there they settled the farther reaches of Polynesia. The eastern part of Polynesia was the last to be inhabited. Easter Island was reached about AD 400, New Zealand and Hawaii not until AD 750 to 1000.

Around the ninth century, Arabs arrived in Oceania and for many generations maintained contact with the settlements they established. The first European to reach Oceania was Magellan (1480–1521). After him came Dutch, Spanish, and English.

## Melanesia

Melanesia takes its name from the Greek word *melanos*, for black. Most of the inhabitants of these islands are the dark-skinned Melanesian-Papuan people. They speak over two hundred languages of Malayo-Polynesian origin. Lying south of the equator, Melanesia includes New Guinea, the Bismarck Archipelago, the Fiji Islands, Vanuatu, New Caledonia, and the Solomon Islands. The culture common to all these islands displays great variety in social systems (both patriarchies and matriarchies are found), styles of traditional houses (including pile dwellings and round dwellings), and earthenware. The Melanesians are tenacious in insisting on their own identity.

New Guinea is the world's second largest island, after Greenland. Lying in the southwest Pacific Ocean northwest of Australia, it is politically divided between Papua New Guinea on the east, and Indonesia on the west. New Guinea is 342,000 square miles (885,780 square kilometers) of landmass, 1,500 miles (2,410 kilometers) long, and 400 miles (640 kilometers) wide. Inhabitants include Melanesians, Papuans, and Negritos.

An independent nation since 1975, Papua New Guinea is a member of the Commonwealth of Nations. It is made up of the eastern half of the island of New Guinea; the Bismarck Archipelago, which comprises more than two hundred islands; the Louisiade Archipelago; the Trobriand Islands and the D'Entrecasteaux Islands; Woodlark Island; and Bougainville, Buka, and other nearby islands. New Britain is the largest island of the Bismarck Archipelago, with an area of 14,150 square miles (36,650 square kilometers). The archipelago also includes New Ireland (about 3,340 square miles or 8,650 square kilometers); Lavongai (about 460 square miles or 1,111 square kilometers); the Duke of York Islands (22 square miles or 57 square kilometers); the smaller islands of the Saint Matthias Group; the Vitu Islands; the Umboi Islands; and the eighteen Admiralty Islands (which, with several smaller islands, form the Manus Province of

Papua New Guinea, some 840 square miles or 2,176 square kilometers). The islands were a German protectorate in 1884, were occupied by Australia in 1914, during World War I, and made a League of Nations mandate in 1921. Invaded by the Japanese army in 1942 and retaken by the Allies in 1944 during World War II, they were placed under Australian administration by the United Nations in 1947. Their total area is about 20,720 square miles (53,665 square kilometers) and their population about 435,000.

Over three hundred tropical islands, about one hundred of them populated, make up the Republic of Fiji, independent since 1970. About half the population of some 740,000 consists of Melanesian indigenous Fijians. Most of the rest are Indian, which has led to significant political and religious strife. Until a military coup in 1987, Fiji was a member of the Commonwealth of Nations. A new constitution in 1990 maintains Fijian parliamentary control.

Vanuatu (the former New Hebrides), an independent republic since 1980, is a group of some seventy forested and fertile tropical islands, most of volcanic origin. Some of the volcanoes are active. Espiritu Santo and Efâte, site of Vila, the capital, are the two largest islands. The population of some 156,000 is predominantly Melanesian and uses several Melanesian languages. The majority of the people are Christian.

New Caledonia and its dependent islands, annexed by France in 1853, have been a French overseas territory since 1946. Lying east of Australia, its total area is 7,358 square miles (19,057 square kilometers). Its population of some 166,000 is roughly 43 percent Papuan, 20 percent Polynesian, Indonesian, and Vietnamese, and the rest European. In 1987 the Melanesians boycotted an election in which the rest of the populace voted to remain part of France. In 1989 France created a new system of government, dividing the territory into three provinces, each with its own assembly. New Caledonia sends a senator and two deputies to the French parliament.

The League of Nations granted the Solomon Islands to Australia as a mandate in 1919. Most of the mountainous and forested islands were occupied by Japan during World War II (1939–1945). (Guadalcanal was the scene of particularly heavy fighting.) Since 1978, most of the islands have been part of an independent constitutional monarchy of some thirty islands (10,639 square miles or 27,555 square kilometers) with a population of almost 330,000, of whom 94 percent are Melanesian. (The Solomon Islands administered by Australia became part of Papua New Guinea in 1975.)

**Micronesia**

Over two thousand islands (*micro* means "small," and most of Micronesia consists of small atolls totaling about 1,055 square miles or 2,732 square kilometers), lying east of the Philippines and generally north of the equator, comprise Micronesia. They include the Northern Marianas, Palau (Belau), the Marshall Islands, Tuvalu, Kiribati, Nauru, and the Federated States of Micronesia. This was part of the United Nations Trust Territory of the Pacific Islands in 1947, under the United States. The Security Council ended the trusteeship in 1990, and

Bronze statuette, made on the Trobiand Islands (Melanesia)

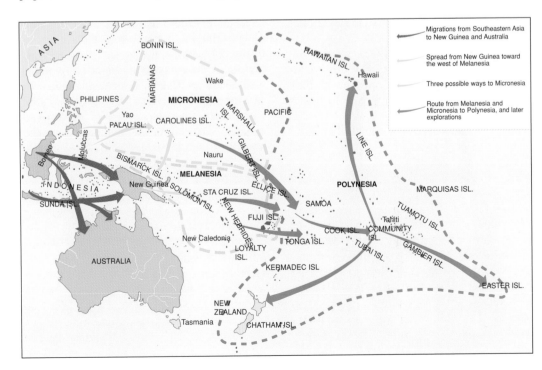

One theory of dissemination is that the inhabitants of the Pacific originally came from eastern Asia. This map shows how it could have taken place.

393

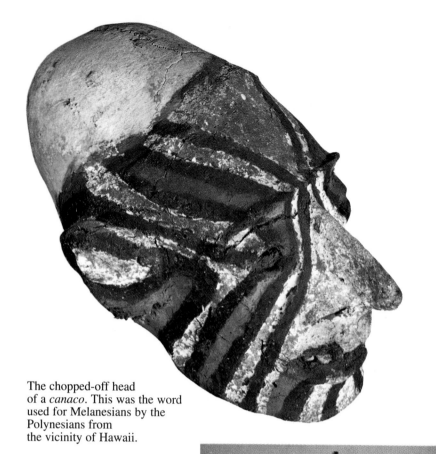

The chopped-off head of a *canaco*. This was the word used for Melanesians by the Polynesians from the vicinity of Hawaii.

admitted the federation to the United Nations in 1991. It has an area of 271 square miles (702 square kilometers) and a population of about 110,000.

Micronesians are usually of Australoid and Polynesian descent, quite different physically from the Melanesians, with whom their culture has much in common.

Early Micronesians were renowned for their knowledge of the sea and the weather. They drew navigation maps on sheets of bark and tapioca fiber that could still be used today. Before the Chinese had invented the compass, these people negotiated long sea voyages. They were the first to travel in dugout canoes equipped with outriggers.

## Polynesia

Polynesia comprises the Hawaiian Islands, Samoa, Tonga, the Marquesas Islands, French Polynesia, and Easter Island. New Zealand might be included because of the Maori, a Polynesian people, dwelling there. Ethnologists have tried to reconstruct the ancient history of Polynesia from its oral tradition, archaeological finds, and anthropological studies of its culture. The population is most likely southeast Asian in origin, although the twentieth-century ocean voyages of Thor Heyerdahl have proven that simple rafts could have made the journey from South America to the Polynesian Islands. He replicated ancient rafts with his own, called *Kon-Tiki*, and followed the path they would have taken.

The twelfth-century AD Polynesian seafarers had a powerful tradition of oral history. Tales from this period have remained alive in epic poems from generation to generation. With the exception of Easter Island, these people never developed a written language. Thanks to the formidable memories of the Polynesians, the poems give a reliable picture of the complex immigration patterns to the various islands. Genealogies and lists of kings kept by people living in isolation from each other for centuries correspond exactly. They describe details about the houses of their homeland and a huge temple with many rooms that served as gathering places for the gods.

Wooden statue from Melanesia

Painted wooden ❯
statue, made in New Guinea.
It portrays the god
of fertility.

Wooden statue of Tangaroa, the Polynesian god of the sea. This statue was found on Easter Island.

Some Polynesian stories are about Java, which can probably be identified as the mythological country called Avaiki, where souls go after death. There are descriptions of snakes, large reptiles, and other animals unknown in Polynesia but found on Java. Maori legends tell of an animal much like a tiger that eats human beings. They also describe a monster covered with scales, with huge long jaws and a powerful tail that suggests the crocodile. The hero in another tale reports seeing creatures "who knew nothing of fire, lived in trees, had big bodies and small heads, and were not people," probably a reference to the orangutans of Borneo.

Tangaroa, hero of Polynesian myth, great god of the ocean, reminisces about a previous stay on Java where he discovered the breadfruit tree. It bears the fruit that replaced rice in the Polynesian diet. The breadfruit tree completely changed the life of Tangaroa's people. Once it was discovered, they no longer planted rice. Tangaroa's son Maui was the first great seafarer of the Pacific. The legends say that Maui "opened the heavens," that he traveled east, toward the rising sun, enabling his people to leave the overpopulated Indonesian islands.

It was supposedly during Maui's lifetime that the Polynesians reached the Fiji Islands, Samoa, Hawaii, and Tahiti. Here, they had no enemies, not even dangerous animals. The land produced fruit and vegetables in great abundance with little effort on their part. Polynesian legends speak of many voyages of discovery. They "visited every corner of the world" and "became skilled in seafaring." Some islands were discovered several times. Hawaii was first visited around AD 650, but it was not colonized until much later. New Zealand was claimed as a possession about 1350, but occasional expeditions had touched there much earlier. According to the epics, a seventh-century navigator set out to surpass the deeds of the legendary seafarer Ivi-te-rangiora. He may have reached Antarctica, where he saw "an animal shaped like a woman that lives in the water" (perhaps a seal) and "a thick sea" (ice floes).

The Polynesians traveled an area as much as 5,000 nautical miles (9,266 kilometers) in different types of canoes. For long expeditions they used a double boat, tying a large canoe to a small one by means of a wooden bridge, on which they stored provisions for the voyage. This singular design gave the whole craft great stability. These canoes were built of planks fastened to a keel carved from a tree trunk. Polynesian tales make frequent mention of the art of repairing canoes in the course of an ocean voyage.

Some Polynesian canoes were 100 feet (30

The head of one
of the large *moai* statues
that were found on
Easter Island

The Polynesian war god.
This wooden statue was found
in a sanctuary on
Hawaii.

meters) long, quite capable of transporting large numbers of warriors. During the expedition to New Zealand in 1350, several hundred people traveled in six canoes. The rations on board were mainly processed breadfruit, which could stay fresh for at least a year, and coconuts, which provided both food and drink. Water was brought in bamboo casks. The Polynesians navigated by the stars, but they were also familiar with prevailing winds and ocean currents. Some kept charts of ocean currents drawn on pieces of wood. Once at sea, the Polynesians made use of the color and temperature of the water to set their course.

## The Riddle of Easter Island

The megalithic monuments of the Polynesians are relatively few in number. They commonly have little decoration and do not bear witness to any great skill in stoneworking. But there is one great exception: the colossal statues of Easter Island. Named after the Easter Sunday on which it was dis-

397

covered by Europeans, Easter Island is 46 square miles (119 square kilometers), located in the South Pacific Ocean 2,000 miles (3,218 kilometers) west of Chile, which annexed the island in 1888. On Easter Island hieroglyphs and colossal stone heads have

This relief, which was carved in a rock, depicts a birdman and presumably has a religious origin.
It was discovered on Easter Island.

been found, some weighing over 50 tons (45.4 metric tons). According to archaeological evidence, the mysterious heads, with their similar faces, were carved over several centuries after AD 1100, while masonry remains found on Easter Island date back to AD 300. Hundreds of these statues stand on

Wooden statue
from Easter Island

the slopes of the extinct volcano Rano Raraku; several hundred more are strewn over great temple plateaus along the coasts. These have occupied scholars for more than two centuries. Was it lack of wood that inspired the Easter Islanders to become involved in the artistic carving of stone?

Easter Island was discovered in 1722 by the Dutch explorer Jacob Roggeveen. (He was disappointed because he had hoped to find the legendary Southland.) In 1770 it was visited by Spaniards; in 1774 by the famous English explorer James Cook; and in 1786 by a Frenchman named La Perouse.

In the nineteenth and twentieth centuries, many scholars sought to solve the mystery of Easter Island. Numerous theories were published about how a simple people could transport huge stone statues weighing many tons. Though this mystery remains unsolved, the 1956 *Kon-Tiki* expedition of the Norwegian Thor Heyerdahl at least shed light on some of the questions about transportation, with his craft's ability to withstand a long seagoing journey.

### Red-haired Easter Islanders

Easter Island is about 2,000 miles (3,218 kilometers) from the South American coast and more than 1,000 miles (1,609 kilome-

ters) from the nearest island. When it was discovered, 4,000 people lived there, but plagues spread by the Europeans, forced labor, and oppression had left only ninety inhabitants by the mid-1800s. Their number has risen to seven or eight hundred at present. The population appears to be Polynesian and their language is related to the other Polynesian tongues. On the island, however, there are also a few very light-skinned, red-haired families. This leads anthropologists to think that they may be the descendants of an older race that came from South America, because red-haired rulers and nobles also existed among the Incas. Heyerdahl theorized that these red-headed people were the carvers of the mysterious great heads.

Whoever created them, it is assumed that the gigantic stone images are portraits of people who once played an important role in the life of the Easter Islanders. They must be more than mere portraits of ancestors. The effort it took to make and transport them points to their part in religious rituals. Perhaps they are portraits of the "birdmen." On the windswept, barren island, the eggs of sea birds were a vital supplement to the monotonous menu. Every year, a contest was held to see who would be the first to bring

The British explorer James Cook (1728–1779) arrives on Malekula (one of the New Hebrides) during his second voyage of discovery.

399

Maori amulet
that was worn to give
protection against
witchcraft

back an egg from one of the islands where the birds nested across from Easter Island. The winner was made a dignitary, a sort of king-priest credited with extensive powers. He was pictured on the rocks wearing a mask like a bird's beak. His exalted position lasted for the year, until the next winner took his place. He was then immortalized in a statue, which did not attempt to be a realistic portrait. All the Easter Island images are similar, except in size.

## Language and Symbols

Even today the riddles of Easter Island have not been satisfactorily solved. Who were the people with red hair who were found there by the first Europeans? Had their ancestors crossed long ago from South America on great rafts, as Heyerdahl believed? Did they then become the victims of a new invasion by dark-haired, "short-eared" Polynesians? Did these newcomers exterminate them and overthrow their images? How is it possible that a written language emerged among the

Polynesians only on this small, isolated island? Was it an invention of the fair-haired people, and is that why none of the later islanders were still capable of deciphering it? The writing of Easter Island is a pictorial language. Although it did not at first look difficult to decipher, because it contained clearly identifiable images of people, fish, canoes, and birds, the texts remain largely incomprehensible. Today, many scholars

think that it was developed to facilitate ritualistic chanting, with each image a key word in the larger context. The writing, it is thought, was not particularly intended to remain a secret, though it has, through our inability to understand it.

At the end of the nineteenth century old Polynesian men who claimed to have learned the script in school would spend hours reading the lines on a single tablet. Their stories were full of repetitions and epic turns of phrase. This may indicate that the Polynesians took over the secret writing of their predecessors and gave it a symbolic meaning of their own.

## Cannibalism in Polynesia
It was a great shock to the European discoverers of Polynesia in the eighteenth century, with their enthusiasm for the people they

Inhabitants of
New Zealand in a prow,
as seen through the
eyes of Louis-Isidore Duperrey.
Engraving from his book
*A Voyage around the
World*

encountered, to discover that some of them practiced cannibalism. Apparently it was a custom in much of Polynesia; the explorer Captain James Cook himself was one of its victims. To the western mind it did not seem reconcilable with the great hospitality and generosity of the Polynesians. It is said that on Samoa it was customary to wrap a captive in palm leaves, as if he were about to be roasted, and to present him to the ruler in this condition. This custom may have been motivated by revenge, as a way of finally destroying an enemy, or as a means of incorporating his strength. The Maoris in New Zealand, for instance, ate certain parts of a decapitated enemy in order to acquire the power of his *mana* (spirit).

## Legends

Oral tradition in Oceanic cultures is such that old people have been known to give precise accounts of events that had taken place 500 years earlier. Epic poems recorded from oral traditions frequently recount gruesome battles between rival clans. The causes of these feuds were usually trivial, but their consequences were appalling. Entire island populations were exterminated.

The story of Princess Apakura of Rarotonga serves as a good example. Her ten brothers were jealous of her son, said to be the handsomest young man on the island. They demanded that he be sacrificed. After his death, his mother asked her relatives from a second island, and then a third, to help avenge him. The legend says that the parties fought on the beach "for seven days and seven nights." Only when the brother who had instigated the sacrifice was killed did the feud end. Another son of Apakura was then chosen to reign in Rarotonga.

## Lyric and Epic Poetry

Polynesian tales teem with interesting details and mysterious events. Stories were often embroidered with supernatural phenomena. The songs occasionally reached great lyrical and dramatic heights. Some developed into hymns of praise that lasted for days. In most cases, the historical core of the tale was always kept intact. The legends describe a fascinating world that was largely destroyed by the arrival of the Europeans.

Below is a passage from the epic of Tavahiki, in which the hero searches the Pacific islands for the mortal remains of his father: "The rainbow appeared on the path of Tavahiki. Tavahiki followed its course. Tavahiki rowed straight, by memory, to Tane, under the influence of the eyes of Kariki, moving under beams of light that shone upon the men and the canoes."

Another hero, driven from his home by civil war, takes the following farewell of his beloved island: "Great is my love for you, my dear land; great is my love for Tahiti, which I now am leaving. Great is my love for the holy temples, my love for the Pure-Ora that I now must leave. Great is my love for the spring where I used to drink, the clear Vaikura-Mata, which I shall see no more. Great is my love for the house that I am leaving, Rapa that I must leave behind. Oh, the river in which I swam and the mountains of my island that I climbed!"

Wooden
Maori statue

402

Cave painting of a man, a woman, and a child from Jabbaren in the Tassili N'Ajjer in Algeria, Africa. The painting dates from the seventh to the first millennia BC.

# Africa *Early History*

## Topography

The continent of Africa is marked by three major plateaus and deserts that did not exist 10,000 years ago. The Sahara runs 3,000 bleak miles (4,830 kilometers) across the top of the Northern Plateau, edging northwest into semiarid steppes and the Atlas Mountains. Lake Chad, only 4 feet (1.2 meters) in average depth, lies at the center of this plateau. The Mediterranean renders a narrow coastal fringe of the continent mild and humid, where the Phoenicians established the empire of Carthage before 700 BC.

The fertile plateau of the eastern highlands divides the Sahara from the Horn Desert. The highlands run down the Indian Ocean coast, from the Red Sea to the Zambezi River. They include the Ethiopian Plateau, the highest part of Africa, rising from an average of 5,000 feet (1,500 meters) to the peak of Ras Dashan, 15,157 feet (4,620 meters) high. South of that range are the volcanic peaks of Mount Elgon, Mount Kenya, and Mount Kilimanjaro, the highest mountain in Africa. (It has two peaks: Kibo at 19,340 feet, or 5,895 meters, and Mawensi at 16,892 feet, or 5,149 meters above sea level.)

The foothills of Kilimanjaro slope west to the Serengeti Plain and Lake Victoria, largest lake in Africa and the third largest in the world. The Olduvai Gorge, almost 300 feet (91 meters) deep, cuts the eastern Serengeti

403

for some 30 miles (50 kilometers). Layers of deposits found in its walls (by archaeologists Louis and Mary Leakey and others) have provided more information about the physical evolution of humankind than any other single source. Fossils of early hominids (humanlike creatures), stone tools, and building sites over two million years old have been discovered.

The Great Rift Valley slashes the eastern highlands, running 3,000 miles (4,830 kilometers) from Syria to southeastern Africa. The Nile River rises in those highlands and flows through a chain of lakes in the Rift Valley, 4,132 miles (6,650 kilometers) north to the Mediterranean. The Ruwenzori Range lies just west of the lakes, reaching an elevation of 16,795 feet (5,119 meters).

The vast grassy plain of the Sudan, far wider and more forested in early continental history than now, lies south of the Sahara. Below it, tropical rain forests line the western and southern coasts of the Gulf of Guinea. The continent's third longest river, the Niger, drains this region. Originating in the western highlands of the Futa Jallon, it flows about 2,600 miles (4,180 kilometers) north and east, then south to empty into the Gulf of Guinea. Like all of Africa's rivers, it has a series of cataracts that limit navigation. The Congo River Basin lies in central Africa on the Central and Southern Plateau. More than 1.6 million square miles (4.1 million square kilometers) in area, its dense equatorial rain forest is drained by the Congo River, at 2,900 miles (4,670 kilometers) long, the second longest river in Africa. It flows generally north to Stanley Falls, then winds its way to the South Atlantic Ocean. The Congo headwaters, like those of the Zambezi River, are on the Katanga Plateau, part of the Central and Southern Plateau. The Zambezi, about 2,200 miles (3,540 kilometers) in length, flows south and east over the spectacular Victoria Falls to the Indian Ocean. The Orange River and its tributary, the Vaal River, drain southern Africa, flowing some 1,300 miles (2,100 kilometers) from the southeastern Drakensberg Mountains to the Atlantic.

View of the
Sahara Desert in the south
of Algeria

African cave painting depicting a bison hunt

Farther south on the Central and Southern Plateau are the 275,000 square miles (712,250 square kilometers) of the Kalahari Desert. Most of it is arid red soil, but it turns to expanses of sand in the east. The peoples of the Khoikhoi and the San (once called Bushmen) inhabit it, as they have for thousands of years. West of it lies the temperate Namib Desert, which extends 1,200 miles (1,930 kilometers) along the southwestern coast of the continent. The Namib, 100 miles (160 kilometers) wide, is cooled by the offshore Benguela Current. Like the Sahara, the Horn, the Kalahari, and the arid Karroo Plateau at the tip of Africa, it receives only some 10 inches (25 centimeters) of rain each year.

### Madagascar

Madagascar, the fourth largest island in the world, with an area of 226,658 square miles (587,041 square kilometers), lies off the

Agriculture, livestock breeding, and metalworking were introduced in Africa several millennia before the Christian era. This photo shows a modern livestock farmer from Kenya with his herd.

405

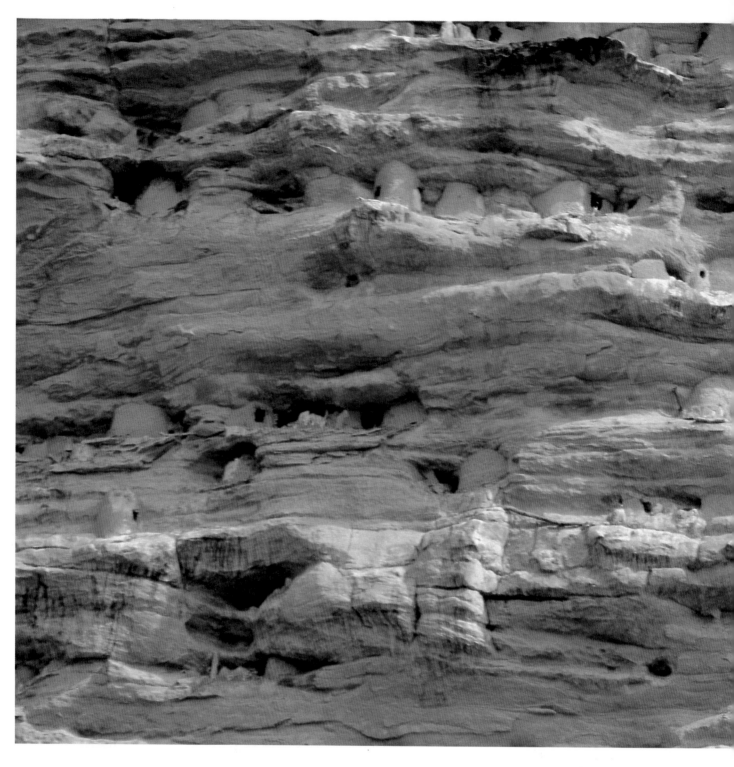

The many natural caves in the falaise of Bandiagara, a steep cliff face that stretches 162.5 miles (260 kilometers) in the republic of Mali, have been in use by people from the third to second centuries BC. From the eleventh to fifteenth centuries the Tellem people lived at the base of the cliff, using the caves for the storage of food, the burial of their dead, and maybe as a place of refuge in times of war. The Tellem people became extinct in the fifteenth century AD, and the caves have been named after them.

southeastern coast of Africa. The land rises from coastal plains to an elevation of 8,671 feet (2,643 meters) in the Ankaratra Mountains. The rugged central highland, once covered with evergreen and deciduous forests, has a seasonal temperate climate. The coastal regions stay summerlike all year. Rainfall patterns vary greatly, from 120 inches (3 meters) brought to the southeast by the trade winds to less than 15 inches (38 centimeters) in the arid south and southwest. The island soil is red, composed of ironstone (murrum) and the brick-colored stone laterite.

## Social Evolution

The first people, *Homo sapiens sapiens*, common ancestors of humanity, began hunting, gathering, and fashioning tools out of stone some 200,000 years ago in Africa.

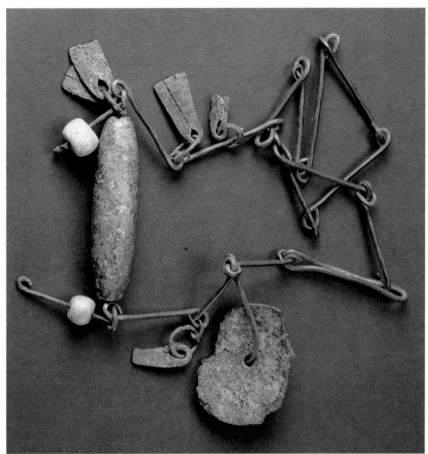

Since the fourteenth and fifteenth centuries the Dogon, an agricultural people, have lived at the base of the falaise of the Bandiagara in Mali. Ritual chains, made from iron and stone beads, are worn by the priests and other religious inhabitants of a village. According to Dogon legend, the beads symbolize the limbs of one of their four forefathers.

Spreading over the continent in nomadic groups, they made bows and arrows by about 15,000 BC.

At about 13,000 BC climatological changes in Northeast Africa led to the gradual extinction of wild animals and the appearance of a new culture based on the gathering of wild grains. Its characteristic tools were stone sickles and grinding stones. The culture spread through North Africa and up the eastern Mediterranean coast to Palestine, Syria, Mesopotamia, and Iran. The people who adopted it would develop the Afro-Asiatic language family. As they sought to control their supply of food, they began to grow plants and to domesticate animals, raising goats, sheep, cattle, and donkeys.

Africa's appearance changed greatly from 9000 to 2000 BC, affected by abundant rainfall. Another way of life appeared in North Africa. Called the water culture, it reached from the Atlantic Ocean to the Nile and southward to the East African lake country. The region had far more lakes, large rivers, and swamps than it does now. Around 8000 BC, San-like (Bushmanoid) hunters and gatherers began to yield the most fertile areas to Negroid peoples who had taken up agriculture and herding. Their ancestors

The Dogon are known for their complex cosmology that is linked with their sculptures. There is a difference in language and sculptural style between the different Dogon groups. This statuette comes from the southern Toro, who make rather abstract sculptures. Statues with a flat head served as an altar for offerings; the thick covering layer consists of dried offerings.

407

The baobab trees
are characteristic of the
African landscape

developed the Nile-Sahara languages and a complex culture that manufactured pottery. The various techniques they used to collect food were evidently so successful as to permit the establishment of fixed settlements. There is also archaeological evidence of temporary camps that served specific purposes: the gathering of certain seasonal crops, the making of tools, or hunting.

Racial characteristics evolved about 10,000 BC. (Some 3,000 ethnic groups have been distinguished.) By the end of the late Stone Age, in 3000 BC, two cultures had developed: the Sango of the rain forests and

the Stillbay of the drier marginal areas. The groups were familiar with the same tools, but there are clear anatomical differences in their skeletal remains.

Another group, the Pygmies, averaging heights of under 5 feet tall (1.5 meters), ranged the equatorial rain forests of the Congo River Basin. Their descendants are there today. (Genetically distinct non-African Pygmies, probably also of archaic origin, live in Asia and Oceania.)

At around 2000 BC the wet period ended, and within two hundred years the Sahara became a great desert. (That process of

A hack, used for the
working of the land. The shape
of this instrument has not
changed since the days
of early agriculture.

desertification continues today, as the Sahara encroaches on the region below it, the Sahel.) As the Nile-Sahara and the African-Asiatic societies adapted their food-gathering techniques to the drier enviroment, two important ecological factors determined the further development of their agriculture: the amount of rainfall and the fertility of the soil. The least labor-intensive crops with the greatest food yield were the ones cultivated. The kinds of crops varied with the region, determining the principal dietary ingredients. New technologies and social systems appeared as the masters of agriculture replaced the nomadic hunters and gatherers.

## Use of Metal
Bronze, an alloy of copper and tin, was produced and used to a limited degree in North Africa around 2000 BC, but the continent as a whole never experienced a Bronze Age. Around the turn of the first millennium a large copper industry flourished in southern Zaire, but iron had by then become the most important metal. Iron was in use around 700 BC on the lower Nile (brought there by the Assyrians) and in Carthage (carried by the Phoenicians who established that colony on the Mediterranean). It would be manufactured by the Cush Empire on the middle Nile some two hundred years later. The continent's earliest known iron culture, Nok Village, lay on the Bauchi Plateau between Lake Chad and the Gulf of Guinea in West Africa. Iron (and sculptured terra-cotta heads) recovered there date from 440 BC to AD 200. The use of iron was widespread among other cultures in East and Central Africa beginning about AD 200.

## Social Organization
On the basis of anthropological studies of present-day peoples who are hunters and gatherers, certain assumptions can be made with regard to these early societies. Strong social bonds aimed at preserving the group would have existed. Communal sharing and equality, based on individual ability, would have been important values. Decisions would likely have been reached by negotiation rather than imposed by recognized leaders.

The obtaining of food, whether by hunting or the gathering of plants, would have been systematically divided, often between the sexes, with the men hunting and the women gathering. If newer social patterns are any indication, hunting would have been seen as more important and the men accorded higher status.

As the transition to an agrarian lifestyle began, new social guidelines probably evolved. New forms of social organization facilitating the management of the larger groups now living in permanent settlements would have developed. Groups of people would have begun to be managed on the basis of collective identity, descent from a common

ancestor. Judging by current customs in Africa, genealogy would have been traced from either a man or a woman. (Anthropologists call this patrilinear or matrilinear descent.) As lineage played an increasingly important role in the organization of food production and society, leaders, especially the elderly, gained status. Marriage arrangements no doubt became important factors in economic and political relations.

Painted wooden statue, made by one of the tribes of the Yoruba in Nigeria

409

In many cultures the birth of a twin is a special occasion. The Yoruba in Nigeria even have a cult to honor the memory of deceased twins. When a twin child has died, a wooden statue, called *ibeji*, is ceremonially handed to its mother. The statuette then gets its own place within the family, and in this way the dead child will stay present.

## Communication

As people evolved from roaming bands of hunters to gatherers of the abundant natural resources around them to manipulators of that environment, they developed new ways to communicate. One of the earliest peoples, the San, who were socially organized into small independent groups, left a legacy of painted and carved rock over most of the southern half of Africa.

The trade routes through the Sahara were communication channels of great importance. Cave paintings discovered at Tassili in West Africa show travel along them carried on by oxcart. A transportation revolution occurred in the first century AD with the introduction of the camel from Asia. Since the camel is able to survive without water for ten days or more and travels considerably faster than the ox, it became a major factor in trans-Sahara trade.

The achievements of the agrarian groups, some of which had the ability to produce iron, spread through migration, fostered by a search for new land and fueled by power struggles over territory considered valuable for various purposes. They organized themselves into units of increasingly larger size. Political leaders arose in response to social needs and became increasingly important as the early African kingdoms developed.

## Bantu Migration

In the first millennium BC, the Bantu people, part of the dominant agricultural group, began a migration, one of the largest in human history, that lasted through the fourth century AD. Linguistic evidence suggests that they moved south from their original homeland in the lower Niger region. They divided linguistically into eastern and western branches. The Eastern Bantu migrated through what is now Zimbabwe, crossing the Limpopo River into South Africa. Their descendants include the Shona, the Xhosa, the Kikuyu, and the Zulu. The Western Bantu moved down the coast and inland, becoming the ancestors of today's Herero and Tonga people.

The Bantu brought their cattle with them, no longer slaughtered for meat. Excellent breeders of livestock, they fed on cow milk and blood. They also brought techniques of farming and ironmaking which allowed them to dominate less-advanced indigenous cultures. They probably learned their ironmaking from the Nok people. Descendants of the Bantu, considered more a language group than a cultural entity, would build kingdoms in much of Africa.

## Languages and Cultures

Bantu is part of the Niger-Kordofanian linguistic family, largest of the four language families in Africa. Each language family is divided by linguists into branches using related but separate languages. Although there are more than a thousand languages in Africa, fifty of which are used by more than 500,000 people, most are used by about 200,000 people. Writing systems exist for only about half of these languages. Noted for their ancient oral traditions, most groups have no written literature. Their alphabets were created by missionaries who adapted the Roman alphabet to the sounds and meanings they interpreted. The Vai people of Liberia and the Bamum of Cameroon, however, have devised their own syllabic writing systems.

An alphabet is an attempt to supply unique symbols for separate sounds. A syllabary system represents several spoken sounds (pronounced as a unit) with a single symbol. A pictographic system uses pictures to represent the objects drawn. The names of the pictures are the words. (A drawing of a lion, for example, would represent the word for that animal.) An ideographic system is more complex, combining pictographs to explain concepts rather than objects.

### Khoisan

The Bantu displaced the indigenous hunting and gathering peoples of the San (Bushmen) and Khoikhoi (Hottentot). Both peoples adopted aspects of their culture but retained their own unique language, Khoisan, smallest of the African-language families. Khoisan is called the Click language, characterized by the distinctive click sounds (made by the tongue position) that begin many words. It is spoken today by some 100,000 people, primarily the Khoikhoi and San who still frequent southern Africa. (Some 25,000 people in Tanzania, however, also speak related Sandawe and Hadza.)

### Niger-Kordofanian

As the Bantu-speaking peoples settled Africa, they left a legacy of languages among the Niger-Kordofanian family that are spoken by three out of four Africans today. One of its two subfamilies is Niger-Congo, divided into several branches. Its linguistic area covers virtually all of Africa below the Sahara. The other Niger-Kordofanian subfamily, Kordofanian, is used only in southern Sudan. Despite the fact that these languages developed in widely separated regions over 5,000 years, they have many similar words.

Languages of the Niger-Kordofanian fam-

According to the Yoruba, many psychological and physical diseases are the result of witchcraft, and the healers have the task of protecting people against it. Yoruba herbalists and healers carry iron healer's staffs crowned with birds. The small birds symbolize witches and their black magic powers. The large bird symbolizes the god of prophesy, and is placed above them to show that sickness and death can be overcome.

ily are spoken today by over 160 million people. Up to 50 million of them on the east coast speak the Bantu-derived trade language Swahili. Other major languages in the northeast include Sukuma in Tanzania, Kikuyu in Kenya, and Ganda in Uganda. (In

411

View of the setting
sun above the River Niger
in Mali

1995 the speakers of Rwanda in Rwanda and
Rundi in Burundi vied for regional suprema-
cy.) In the southeast, Bantu derivatives
include Zulu and Xhosa in South Africa;
Makua in Mozambique; Nyanja in Malawi;
Shona in Zimbabwe; and Bemba in Zambia.
Elsewhere, they are Kimbundu and
Umbundu in Angola; Fang and Bulu in
Cameroon; and Ngala and Kongo in the
Congo and Zaire.

Although Bantu is the largest branch of
the Niger-Congo subfamily, there are others
of importance. These include the West
Sundanic, the Ijo, the Gur, and the oldest
branch, the Mande. Fula (of the nomadic
cattle-herders, the Fulani) is the most widely
spoken language of another branch, the West
Atlantic. Languages of the Kwa branch
(Efik, Igbo, and Yoruba) were a factor in the
Nigerian war in 1960. The branch includes
Ewe, Fanti, Twi, Anyi, Baule, and Liberias
Bassa and Kru.

### Nilo-Saharan

Nilotic peoples migrated to the inland inter-
lacustrine (interlake) region, following the
rivers south and carrying language with
them. The Nilo-Saharan languages developed and are still found, as their name
implies, in the upper Nile Valley, the Sudan,
the Sahara, and in East Africa. Spoken today
by more than 160 million people, Nilotic
languages include Dinka, Nuer, Shilluk, and
Luo. This is the language family of two large
cattle-based cultures, the Nuer and the
Masai. The Nuer watch their herds in the
swamps and plains of southern Sudan. The
Masai move theirs seasonally on the high
plains of Tanzania and Kenya. The ancient
related tongue of Songhai is still spoken in
the reaches of the Niger River.

Alone among living African languages
before the modern era, only Nilo-Saharan
Nubian developed a literature. Religious
documents written in it, dating from the
eighth to the fourteenth centuries, have been
recovered. The Nubian alphabet they used
stemmed from the Coptic.

## Hamito-Semitic

The Hamito-Semitic (or Afro-Asiatic) family includes Arabic and the Semitic languages of Asia and Africa. In the narrow fertile valley of the Nile River, the farming villages formed about 5000 BC are the oldest indigenous culture of Africa. Around 3500 BC they developed into independent kingdoms, unified by Menes, the first pharaoh of Egypt, about 3000 BC. Ancient Egyptian, written in hieroglyphics, constituted its own branch of the Hamito-Semitic language family. No living languages are derived from it. However, 160 million people in northern Africa today speak some Hamito-Semitic language.

Semitic people crossed the Red Sea from Sheba in southern Arabia over the first millennium BC. They merged with the Hamite people they found on the coast, amassing an extensive body of language and a varied culture. Ethnologists dispute exactly who the Hamites were, but generally agree they were Caucasian. Whatever their origin, the Hamites were receptive to outside influences at least in part because of their favorable location for trade. Situated on the Red Sea and the Gulf of Aden, the Hamite domain and the Red Sea port of Adulis constituted a natural stopping place for trade ships sailing between Egypt and the Mediterranean, India, and the Far East. The Hamites included the ancient Egyptians; the coastal Afar, the Oromoto; the Guanche of the Canary Islands; the Berber who inhabited northwest-

Entrance in one of the walls overlooking the temple complex of the great ruins in Zimbabwe. The walls were built without the use of cement.

View of the temple in the great ruins of Zimbabwe. Within its walls Arab and Chinese ceramics have been found.

413

ern Africa before pharaonic times; and the Tuareg, Fula, and Tibbu peoples of the Sahara. All of these peoples developed their own languages.

The Cushitic branch of Afro-Asiatic is spoken in the Ethiopian Highlands, along the Red Sea, and on the Horn of Africa. The ancient tongue of the Amhara people, called Amharic, is the official language of Ethiopia. That country's hallmark work of literature, *Kebra'nagast* (*The Glory of the Kings*), is written in the ancient language of Gecez, which is no longer spoken. Gecez literature

Many luxury utensils of the Kuba in Zaire are made of richly decorated and carved wood, like this box that is used for the storage of *tukula*, or red dye powder. This powder is used in rituals for the coloring of masks, statues, and people. Women also mix *tukula* with soil and oil, and make so-called *bongoto* figurines that are prominent in mourning ceremonies.

also includes several unique books of the Christian Apochryphal tradition.

Major Cushitic languages also include Galla (spoken by the Oromoto) and Danakil, spoken by the nomadic sheep-herding Afar people of the Danakil Depression. At 381 feet (116 meters) below sea level, this is one of the hottest regions on earth. The people of Eritrea, one of Africa's oldest cultures and newest nations, speak the related Tigrinya and Tigre. (Bordering on the Red Sea between Djibouti and Ethiopia, touching the nation of Sudan on the north and northwest, Eritrea has been variously under Italian, British, and Ethiopian control. After prolonged war it finally achieved independence in 1993.)

The Cushite people called the Somali (also the name of their language) migrated to the Horn of Africa from Yemen in the thirteenth century, encountering Arab tribes that had settled there six centuries earlier. The region that is now Somalia was familiar to ancient

Egyptians as Punt. Ethiopians made it part of the kingdom of Aksum from the second to the seventh centuries AD. Independent Somali kings battled for control in the sixteenth century, beginning a long history of ethnic turmoil that continues in the 1990s.

The Berbers frequented the High Atlas Mountains and the steppes of northwestern Africa before 3000 BC. The Berber branch of the Hamito-Semitic family is spoken today in much of the same region and on the southwestern edge of the Sahara. The Berbers established the Almoravid dynasty that ruled there and in parts of Spain in the eleventh and twelfth centuries AD. Arabic-speaking Bedouins entered Africa from the Arabian Peninsula over that same period. They brought with them a migratory lifestyle, dependent on camels and flocks of goats and sheep that overgrazed the land, upsetting the Berber ecological balance.

The Berber language, Tamarshak, is spoken and written by the Tuareg, tribal people of the Sahara, who have devised their own alphabet. They once controlled most of the Sahara, taxing caravans and raiding neighboring tribes for slaves. Affected by the French conquest of Algeria, today they try to maintain a nomadic lifestyle (organized by matrilinear descent) in the face of political turmoil.

Ten million people, largely in northern Nigeria, speak the languages of another Hamito-Semitic branch, the Chadic. The predominant Chadic language is Hausa, similar to Swahili in its widespread use in trade and education. The Hausa wrote an extensive historical literature, using the Arabic alphabet. They established strong kingdoms oriented to commerce before the tenth century. These were Biram, Daura, Zaria, Rano, Gobir, Katsina, and Kano, the last two built into major trade centers in the sixteenth century.

### Malagasy

Malagasy, the language spoken on Madagascar (in addition to the French brought by its colonizers), reflects its origin as a member of the Malayo-Polynesian group. The island was settled before AD 1000, and its culture, as well as its language, is Southeast Asian in origin. It was blended with African and followed later by Arab and European influences.

# TIME LINE

| | THE PHOENICIANS POLITICAL HISTORY | THE PHOENICIANS CULTURAL HISTORY | EVENTS IN THE REST OF THE WORLD |
|---|---|---|---|
| **BC**<br>2500 | **2500** Canaanites reach the east coast of the Mediterranean Sea | **c.2500** Phoenicians divide into tribes | **c.2500** Indus Valley cities of Harappa and Mohenjo-Daro built |
| 2400 | | | |
| 2300 | | | |
| 2200 | | | |
| 2100 | | | |
| 2000 | **2000** Canaanites from loose federation of city-states and republics; cities governed by a council of elders | **c.2000** Cuneiform tablets illustrate Phoenician religion | **c.2000** Introduction of the horse-drawn chariot by the Hittites |
| 1900 | | | |
| 1800 | | | |
| 1700 | | | |
| 1600 | **1550–1360** Golden Age of the city of Ugarit | **c.1550–1200** Ugarit becomes the major commercial city on the northern Phoenician coast | **c.1550–1270** New Kingdom in Egypt |
| 1500 | | | |
| 1400 | | | |
| 1300 | | | **1290–1224** Ramses II is pharaoh of Egypt |
| 1200 | **c. 1200** Final demise of Ugarit | **c.1250** Development of the Phoenician alphabet | |
| 1100 | | | **c.1027** Zhou dynasty in China |
| 1000 | | | **c.1000** David is crowned king of the people of Israel |
| 900 | **969–936** Hiram I becomes ruler of Tyre<br>**c.850** Hiram's grandson is replaced by the priest of Astarte<br>**814** Foundation of the colony of Carthage | **c.900** Phoenicians trade from Asia Minor to Egypt; from Arabia to southern Spain; their cedar and purple fabric dye in great demand | |
| 800 | | **c.800–700** Adoption of the Phoenician alphabet by the Greeks<br>**c.750–700** Homer mentions Sidonians instead of Phoenicians<br>**c.700–500** Phoenician shipping logs written | **753** Foundation of Rome |
| 700 | | | |
| 600 | | **c.600** Phoenicians sail around Africa | **594** Solon introduces reforms in Athens |
| 500 | | **c.520** Carthage sends an expedition to found colonies beyond Gibraltar, explores the Atlantic coasts | **c.586** The Hebrew people led into Babylonian exile<br>**c.563–483** The Buddha<br>**c.551–479** Confucius (Kong Fuzi) |
| 400 | | | |
| 300 | | | **334–323** Alexander the Great conquers and rules a worldwide empire |
| **AD**<br>150 | | **c.150** The works of Philo of Byblos provide insight into Phoenician traditions | |
| 250 | | **c.250** Phoenician cult of Astarte Tammuz celebrated in Roman towns | |
| 300 | | **c.300** Church father Eusebius uses the works of Philo of Byblos | |

| Prehistory | Antiquity | Middle Ages | Renaissance | Modern History | Contemporary History |
|---|---|---|---|---|---|

| | THE PEOPLE OF ISRAEL POLITICAL HISTORY | THE PEOPLE OF ISRAEL CULTURAL HISTORY | EVENTS IN THE REST OF THE WORLD |
|---|---|---|---|
| **BC** | | | |
| **9000** | **c.9000–2500** Neolithic culture | **c.9000–2500** Neolithic man discovers agriculture | |
| **2500** | **c.2500–2000** Palestine inhabited by Semitic peoples | **c.2500–2000** Mixing of the Semitic peoples with the native Canaanites | **c.2500** Mesopotamia occupied by the Amorites |
| **2400** | | | |
| **2300** | | | |
| **2200** | | | |
| **2100** | | | |
| **2000** | **c.2000–1750** Hebrews migrate into Palestine; Abraham travels to Palestine | | **c.2000–1500** Aramaeans adopt much from the peoples they encounter |
| **1900** | | | |
| **1800** | | | |
| **1700** | **c.1650/1450–1250** Stay of the Israelites in Egypt | **c.1750** Abraham forms covenant with God | |
| **1600** | | **c.1650/1450–1250** Famine drives the people of Israel to the Nile Delta | |
| **1500** | | | **c.1550–1070** New Kingdom in Egypt |
| **1400** | | | **c.1425** Destruction of the palace at Knossos<br>**c.1380** Beginning of the New Empire of the Hittites |
| **1300** | | | **c.1353–1340** Pharaoh Akhenaten<br>**c.1286** Hittites win the battle of Kadesh |
| **1200** | **c.1224–1214** Exodus of the Hebrews from Egypt to Palestine<br>**c.1200** Philistines occupy five coastal cities in Palestine<br>**c.1200–1025** Period of the Judges<br>**c.1180** Gradual occupation of the West Bank of the Jordan | **c.1224–1214** Exodus from Egypt led by Moses, prophet and lawgiver<br>**c.1200** "Ten Commandments"<br><br>**c.1180** Israelites coexist peacefully with surrounding peoples; Canaanite religion is source of temptation for Hebrews | **c.1224–1214** Merneptah pharaoh of Egypt |
| **1100** | | | |
| **1000** | **c.1010** Saul anointed king<br>**c.1000** David chosen as king, start of hereditary monarchy, conquest of Jerusalem<br>**966–926** Solomon forms alliance with the Phoenician traders<br>**926** Division of the kingdom<br>**926–722** Kingdom of Israel<br>**925–587** Kingdom of Judah | **c.1000** Jerusalem becomes the new political and cultural center<br><br>**966–926** Building of the temple in Jerusalem<br><br>**926** Decline of the kingdom, desecration of the temple, rise of the prophets | **c.1027** Zhou dynasty in China<br><br>**c.969–936** Hiram I rules Tyre |
| **900** | | | |
| **800** | | | **814** Foundation of Carthage |
| **700** | **745** Assyrian armies appear regularly in Palestine<br>**725–697** King Hezekiah in Jerusalem<br>**722** Destruction of Samaria by Sargon II<br>**701** Assyrian armies in Palestine and Syria | **760** The prophet Amos curses the people of Israel<br>**c.725** Prophet Isaiah<br><br>**c.701** Religious flowering | **c.750** Start of Greek Archaic era |
| **600** | | **c.600** Prophet Jeremiah | |
| **500** | **586** Jerusalem conquered by the Babylonians, start of Babylonian exile | | **594** Legal reforms in Athens under Solon |

| Prehistory | Antiquity | Middle Ages | Renaissance | Modern History | Contemporary History |
|---|---|---|---|---|---|

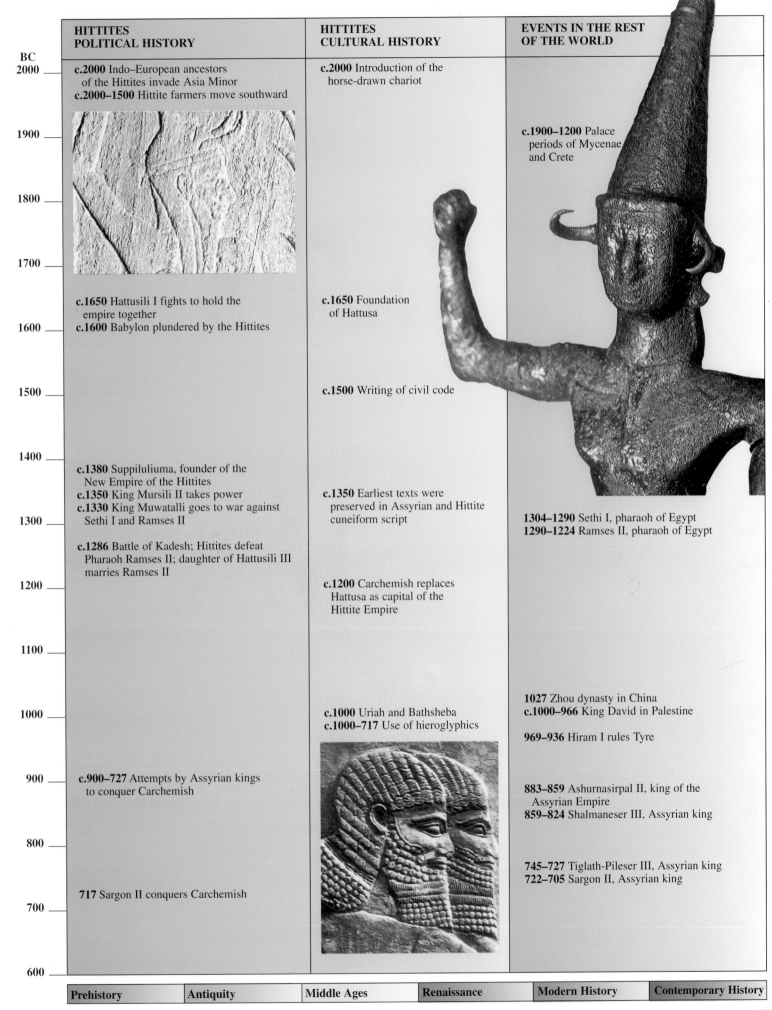

| HITTITES POLITICAL HISTORY | HITTITES CULTURAL HISTORY | EVENTS IN THE REST OF THE WORLD |
|---|---|---|

**BC**

**2000**

**c.2000** Indo–European ancestors of the Hittites invade Asia Minor
**c.2000–1500** Hittite farmers move southward

**c.2000** Introduction of the horse-drawn chariot

**1900**

**c.1900–1200** Palace periods of Mycenae and Crete

**1800**

**1700**

**1650**

**c.1650** Hattusili I fights to hold the empire together
**c.1600** Babylon plundered by the Hittites

**c.1650** Foundation of Hattusa

**1600**

**1500**

**c.1500** Writing of civil code

**1400**

**c.1380** Suppululiuma, founder of the New Empire of the Hittites
**c.1350** King Mursili II takes power
**c.1330** King Muwatalli goes to war against Sethi I and Ramses II

**c.1350** Earliest texts were preserved in Assyrian and Hittite cuneiform script

**1300**

**c.1286** Battle of Kadesh; Hittites defeat Pharaoh Ramses II; daughter of Hattusili III marries Ramses II

**1304–1290** Sethi I, pharaoh of Egypt
**1290–1224** Ramses II, pharaoh of Egypt

**1200**

**c.1200** Carchemish replaces Hattusa as capital of the Hittite Empire

**1100**

**1000**

**c.1000** Uriah and Bathsheba
**c.1000–717** Use of hieroglyphics

**1027** Zhou dynasty in China
**c.1000–966** King David in Palestine

**969–936** Hiram I rules Tyre

**900**

**c.900–727** Attempts by Assyrian kings to conquer Carchemish

**883–859** Ashurnasirpal II, king of the Assyrian Empire
**859–824** Shalmaneser III, Assyrian king

**800**

**745–727** Tiglath-Pileser III, Assyrian king
**722–705** Sargon II, Assyrian king

**700**

**717** Sargon II conquers Carchemish

**600**

| Prehistory | Antiquity | Middle Ages | Renaissance | Modern History | Contemporary History |
|---|---|---|---|---|---|

417

| CHINA POLITICAL HISTORY | CHINA CULTURAL HISTORY | EVENTS IN THE REST OF THE WORLD |
|---|---|---|

**BC**

**c.7000** Neolithic man becomes a farmer

**c.5000** Development of two different neolithic cultures

**c.2200** Legendary dynasty of Xia
**c.2000** Bronze Age of the Shang, first Chinese dynasty

**c.1300** Late Shang state mostly centralized around Anyang

**c.1027** Zhou dynasty subjugates the Shang dynasty
**c.1000** Consolidation of power, growth of the states

**c.700–600** Zhou states involved in internecine battles

**c.500–221** Period of the battling states

**c.400–300** Raids of nomads from the northern steppes

**c.225** Confucius's (Kong Fuzi's) teachings become state ideology
**c.221** Zheng of Qin, first emperor of united China, beginning of the Han dynasty

---

**c.7000** Rye and rice are the major agricultural products
**c.5000** Cultivation of rye and raising of pigs in the north; rice cultivation and husbandry of water buffalo in the south
**c.2500** Agricultural methods develop; manufacture of ceramics; carving of ivory and jade
**c.2000** Manufacture and use of bronze objects, especially in connection with the worship of ancestors; rise of the cities; building of monuments

**c.1450** Complete script on oracle bones

**c.1300** Earliest chariot in China

**c.1000** Feudal states are centralized

**c.600–400** Legalism and Daoism (Taoism)

**c.551–479** Confucius (Kong Fuzi)
**c.550** Chariot replaced by large-scale peasant infantry
**c.500–221** Population growth; intensification of agriculture; growth of market economy based on money; use of iron
**c.450** Introduction of cavalry to the army, chariot becomes a luxurious means of transportation, first written Chinese laws

**c.350** Mencius (Mengzi)

**c.221** The first great wall, end of the feudal system

---

**2000** The horse is used to pull the chariot

**c.1900–1000** Palace period on Crete and Mycenae

**c.1425** Destruction of the palace of Knossos

**1286** Battle of Kadesh

**c.1000** David is made king of the people of Israel

**753** Foundation of Rome by Romulus
**c.750** End of the Dark Ages in Greece

**586** Babylonian exile
**c.563–483** The Buddha
**c.550** Phoenicians sail around Africa
**522** Start of the Persian world empire under Achaemenid ruler Darius I

**334–323** Alexander the Great founds a world empire

**200**

| Prehistory | Antiquity | Middle Ages | Renaissance | Modern History | Contemporary History |
|---|---|---|---|---|---|

| THE PERSIANS POLITICAL HISTORY | THE PERSIANS CULTURAL HISTORY | EVENTS IN THE REST OF THE WORLD |
|---|---|---|
| **c.2500–1500** Indo-European peoples settle east of Mesopotamia up to the Valley of the Indus<br>**c.2000** Indo-European peoples settle on the Persian plateau, strong feudal organization<br><br>**835** Assyrian king Shalmaneser III mentions Persia and Media<br><br>**559–529** Cyrus II conquers the Median Empire<br>**546** Cyrus II defeats Croesus, Lydia becomes a Persian province<br>**539** Conquest of Babylon and the New Babylonian Empire<br>**529** Death of Cyrus II in battle against the Scythians, succeeded by Cambyses<br>**525** Cambyses conquers Egypt<br>**522** Death of Cambyses; noblemen rebel<br>**521–486** Darius I reigns<br><br>**499–494** Revolt of Greek city-states in Ionia against Persian oppression<br>**470** Army of Darius I defeated by the Greeks<br><br>**c.330** Alexander the Great crushes the Persian world empire | **c.2000** The Persians and Indians speak related Indo-European languages. Persians practice animist religious rites with a clear separation between good and evil<br>**c.800–600** Prophet Zarathushtra converts the people; Persians give up nomadic existence for agriculture<br><br>**539** Cyrus allows the Jews to return to Palestine<br><br>**c.522–486** In the Persian world empire, Darius shows high degree of tolerance; rise of Persian art<br>**c.515** Darius I builds a residence in Persepolis<br><br>**c.330** Fire and destruction of Persepolis during its occupation by Alexander the Great | **c.1000** David is made king of the people of Israel<br><br>**610** Medes conquer Nineveh<br>**594** Reforms introduced by Solon in Athens<br>**586** Babylonian exile<br>**560–546** Croesus of Lydia<br>**551–479** Confucius (Kong Fuzi)<br><br>**500–221** Period of battling states in China<br>**478/7** Delian League<br><br>**334–323** Alexander the Great conquers a world empire |

BC — 2500, 2000, 900, 800, 600, 500, 400, 300

| INDIA POLITICAL HISTORY | INDIA CULTURAL HISTORY | EVENTS IN THE REST OF THE WORLD |
|---|---|---|
| **c.2500–1750** Harappa or Indus Valley culture<br><br>**c.2000** Indo–European peoples reach the Indus Valley<br>**c.2000–1700** Indo–Aryans interact with and conquer people of the Indus Valley<br><br><br><br>**513** Indus Valley pays taxes to the Persians<br><br><br>**327** Invasion by Alexander the Great<br><br><br>**325** Greek troops depart to the West<br>**324** Chandra Gupta Maurya creates a power base in Punjab, establishes the Maurya dynasty<br><br>**c.250–232** Golden Age under Asoka | **c.2500** Indus Valley cities of Harappa and Mohenjo–Daro are built; their people have contact with Mesopotamia<br><br>**c.1700** Indo–Aryans introduce a system of social stratification consisting of four castes: priests, warriors, merchants/landowners, and peasants/cultivators/servants<br><br>**c.1500** Earliest sections of Vedas written<br><br>**c.563–483** The Buddha<br><br>**c.540–468** Mahavira<br><br><br>**c.480** Indians fight in the Persian army<br><br><br>**327** Greek colonists in India; rise in trade between Mediterranean and India; mingling of Indian and Greek cultures<br>**327–031** Hellenism, mingling of Indian and Greek cultures<br><br>**c.250** Expansion of contacts with the West | **586** Babylonian exile<br>**551–479** Confucius (Kong Fuzi)<br>**522–486** Darius I<br>**513** Persians conquer the Indus Valley<br>**486–465** Xerxes I in Persia<br>**480–479** Persian campaign against the Greeks<br><br>**334–323** Alexander the Great conquers a world empire<br><br><br>**323–304** Battle of the Diadochs |

BC — 2500, 2000, 1700, 1500, 600, 500, 400, 300, 200

| Prehistory | Antiquity | Middle Ages | Renaissance | Modern History | Contemporary History |
|---|---|---|---|---|---|

| | CULTURES IN THE PACIFIC OCEAN POLITICAL HISTORY | CULTURES IN THE PACIFIC OCEAN CULTURAL HISTORY | EVENTS IN THE REST OF THE WORLD |
|---|---|---|---|
| **BC** 30000 | **30,000–25,000** Settlement of Melanesians on the islands of the Pacific | | |
| 9000 | **c.9000** Melanesians reach Tasmania | | |
| 2500 | **c.2500–1500** Micronesians invade the Pacific Ocean as far as Polynesia | | |
| **AD** 100 | **c.100–1000** People reach the far corners of Polynesia | | |
| 400 | **c.400** Easter Island populated | | |
| 600 | | | **570–632** Prophet Muhammad |
| | **c.650** Polynesians visit Hawaii for the first time | **c.650** Ivi–te–Rangiora, famous navigator | |
| 700 | **c.750–1000** New Zealand and Hawaii populated | | |
| 800 | **c.800–900** Arabs reach Oceania | | **800** Charlemagne the Great crowned emperor |
| 1100 | **c.1100–1200** Golden Age of Polynesian navigators | **c.1100–1200** Polynesian ships made of double canoes, forbidden to women | **1054** Great Schism in the Catholic Church |
| 1300 | | | **1162–1227** Genghis Khan (Chingiz Khan) |
| 1400 | **c.1350** New Zealand discovered and populated by Polynesians | | |
| 1500 | | | **c.1500** Portuguese navigator Magellan is the first European in Oceania |

| | AFRICA POLITICAL HISTORY | AFRICA CULTURAL HISTORY | EVENTS IN THE REST OF THE WORLD |
|---|---|---|---|
| **BC** 13000 | **c.13,000** Gathering of wild grains in the northeast Africa; Afro–Asiatic languages develop | **c.15,000** Invention of bow and arrow **c.13,000** Stone scythe and grinding stone | |
| 9000 | **c.9000–2000** Rise of the water culture | **c.9000–2000** Pottery invented | **c.9000** Melanesians reach Tasmania |
| 8000 | **c.8000** African population consists of hunters and gatherers, slow transition to agrarian society | **c.8000** Strong social ties, no leaders, food distribution | |
| 3000 | **c.3000** Two cultures exist on the continent: Sango and Stillbay | | **c.5000** In China two neolithic cultures evolve |
| 2000 | **c.2000–1800** Sahara becomes a desert | **c.2000** Bronze most important metal **c.2000–1800** New economic and social systems, domestication | **c.2000** Indo-European peoples reach the Indus Valley **c.2000–1750** Hebrews related to the Aramaeans or Israelites migrate into Palestine **c.1600** Babylon razed by the Hittites **c.1550–1070** New Kingdom in Egypt |
| 1000 | **c.1000** Large parts of Africa occupied by the Bantu, Semites, and Hamites | | **c.1027** Zhou dynasty in China **c.1000** David made king of the people of Israel |
| 500 | | **c.500** Knowledge of iron manufacture evolves | |
| **AD** 0 | | **0–100** Rise of copper industry in southern Zaire | |
| 500 | | **c.500** Iron is produced everywhere on the continent | |

| Prehistory | Antiquity | Middle Ages | Renaissance | Modern History | Contemporary History |
|---|---|---|---|---|---|

# Glossary

**Abraham** one of the patriarchs of the Israelites in the Old Testament of the Bible. He moved with his family from the Sumerian city of Ur to Canaan and was said to have been given property rights there by Yahweh in exchange for the promise to worship only Yahweh.

**Achaemenids** Persian dynasty in the ancient Persian kingdom and empire (559–330 BC); whose rulers showed tolerance of the defeated peoples. Cyrus established the empire and Darius expanded it, leaving the subjugated territories autonomous. Alexander the Great conquered this dynasty.

**Adonis** (earlier Tammuz) Phoenician god of vegetation identified with nature's dying in autumn and rebirth in spring. As Adonis he was worshiped by the Greeks and Romans.

**Africa** continent inhabited by a great variety of peoples and cultures, including Semites and Hamites. Hunting tribes such as the Bushmen and Pygmies lived in the interior.

**African Stone Age** Africa was inhabited by civilizations that manufactured increasingly more refined stone tools, e.g., the Olduvai culture (32 million years ago) and the Acheulean culture (1.5 million–100,000 years ago). Language evolved slowly. In about 8000 BC, Africa consisted of communities of hunters and gatherers. Around 3000 BC the Sango culture inhabited the jungle, while the Stillbay culture lived in arid areas.

**Agni** ancient Indian god of fire. He took many forms, including the god of hearth and home and that of the messenger between gods and men who consumed offerings from sacrificial fires and brought them to other gods. He evolved from the prehistoric Indo-Iranian tradition.

**agriculture** (Africa) around 2000 BC most African peoples had moved on to agriculture and cattle breeding. Permanent settlements arose and the population grew, causing a shortage of land.

**Ahura Mazda** supreme god of the Persians. He was the creator and god of truth, justice, and purifying fire. The battle and victory of Ahura Mazda over the evil spirit Angra Mainyu was the foundation of the Persian faith as preached by Zarathushtra.

**Airyana Vaeja** mythological land where both Persians and Indians lived before they separated. It was identified as the first land Ahura Mazda created.

**Aleppo** city in northern Syria on the Euphrates River that was the capital of the kingdom of Yamhad during the eighteenth and seventeenth centuries BC. Its golden age took place at the end of the seventeenth century. It battled the Hittites and was conquered by Mursilis I.

**alphabet** phonetic script with characters for each sound, which the Phoenicians modified and spread to the Greeks, among others. The earliest alphabetic evidence is from the Canaanites in the second millennium BC.

**Amos** Israelite prophet (eighth century BC) who spoke out against social injustice and predicted the fall of the people of Israel, saying that Yahweh would punish them if they did not renounce idol worship.

**Angra Mainyu** evil spirit and symbol of dishonesty, wickedness, and darkness in the religion of Zarathushtra.

**Anyang** capital city of the late Shang period (c.1250) where excavations revealed palaces, temples, living quarters, royal graves, and artisan's workshops. Oracle bones were also found here.

**archives of Boghazköy** (Hattusas) archives of clay tablets found in the ruins of the Hittite capital. They are written in Akkadian and Hittite in the cuneiform script and date from c.1350–1200 BC. They provide information on political history and organization, economy, and religion.

**Aryans** Indo-European peoples who invaded the Indus Valley around 1800 BC and conquered the indigenous peoples. They initially mixed with these native inhabitants, but later dominated them by imposing a system of social stratification that became known as the caste system.

**Ark of the Covenant** repository in which the Ten Commandments and Hebrew desert traditions were kept. It was originally located in Shiloh, but was stolen by the Philistines. Later the Ark was preserved in the Temple in Jerusalem built by Solomon.

**Assyria** ancient kingdom of the Near East, located in northern Mesopotamia. Assyria rose to great power in the early first millennium, established an empire, then collapsed in the seventh century BC.

**Astarte** Canaanite and Phoenician goddess of procreation, fertility, and love. She was equated with the Semitic Ishtar and later associated with the Greek goddess Aphrodite. She was also connected with Baal and was worshiped as the mother-goddess until Roman times.

**Baal** Semitic god of storm and fertility. He was worshiped by the Canaanites and Phoenicians in fertility rites. The Israelites worshiped him as a fertility god.

**Bantu** black people of Africa, south of the equator, who speak related languages. After c.1000 BC they occupied large portions of Africa, leaving the area around Lake Chad and mixing with agricultural peoples.

**birdman** a servant whose master was a king-priest on Easter Island who occupied a chosen position of godlike authority for the term of one year. It was the birdman's obligation to retrieve eggs from the Motu nui.

**Brahmans** highest inherited social status in the Old Indian caste system, consisting of priests and learned men. They spent their time studying and writing the *Vedas*. They were qualified to perform offering ceremonies and teach the *Vedas*.

**Byblos** first city in pre-Phoenician Levant to trade with Egypt. After c.1200 it was superseded as a Phoenician trading center by Sidon and later Tyre. Byblos was the center of the Astarte-Tammuz cult in Roman times.

**Cambyses** king of the Medes and Persians who succeeded his father, Cyrus the Great of the Achaemenid dynasty in 529 or 528. He conquered Egypt in 525 and died in 522.

**Canaanites** Semitic tribes who settled in Palestine and the western Levant in the third millennium and mixed with the native population. They maintained separate city-states. By c.1200 their territory was infiltrated by Israelites and Philistines.

**Carchemish** Hittite city on the Euphrates, an important trading center. After the fall of the Hittite Empire, c.1200, it became the most important Neo-Hittite separate state. Carchemish was conquered by the Assyrians.

**Carthage** trading settlement founded by Phoenician Tyre around 800 BC on the North African coast in Tunisia that became a city and major trading power.

**caste system** social system introduced by the Aryans, who were originally divided into four hereditary strata based on occupation, each with its own rights and obligations. There was no possibility of contact or internal relocation among the castes. The native people were seen as below them and became the pariahs. This still-existing system evolved into numerous new castes and sub-castes.

**Chinese Stone Age** China has been inhabited from the earliest times of humankind. From 7000 BC onward neolithic cultures lived in northern China, where the staple was millet, and in southern China, where rice was the staple. The northern areas were first to evolve into more complex societies.

**Chinese walls** earthen walls built on the northern and western borders of the Zhou states as protection against invading steppe-nomads. Walls were also built between the various Zhou states and around cities, made necessary by the continuous threat of war.

**cows** the Aryans, who were pastoral nomads, considered cows sacred and offered them in sacrifice. The concept of vegetarianism known in the days of the Upanishads (c.600–300 BC) was elaborated on by Buddhists and Jains, who promoted the doctrine of ahimsa, or nonviolence.

**Cyrus** the Great king of Persian Empire from 559 to 530 BC and member of the

421

Achaemenid dynasty. In 558 he obtained hegemony following an uprising against the Medes. In 547 he conquered Lydia and in c.539, the Neo-Babylonian Kingdom.

**Darius** king of the Persian Empire from 521 to 486 BC and member of the Achaemenid dynasty. He created political unity by dividing the empire into twenty satrapies, which were subject to central rule. He consolidated the borders, promoted trade, and developed an infrastructure. He was a follower of Zarathushtra.

**Dark Continent** Western concept from the nineteenth- and twentieth-centuries' study of African history. Because of prejudices and stereotypical ideas concerning the black African population, precolonial Africa was considered primitive and insignificant.

**David** king of Israel and Judah, from c.1000 to 965 BC, successor to Saul. He defeated the Philistines, expanded the kingdom to its greatest size, seized Jerusalem from the Jebusites and made it his capital.

**devas** evil powers in Persian religion. The world was dominated by devas and ahuras, or good spirits, who constantly fought one another. People had to help the ahuras by way of magic formulas, predictions, and offerings.

**dog** dogs enjoyed great respect from the Persians because of their roles in the lives of nomadic cattlemen. They were placed on almost the same level as people.

**Easter Island** easternmost island of Polynesia, colonized around AD 500, the site of hundreds of enormous monolithic statues of mysterious origin.

**exodus** departure of the Israelites from Egypt to Canaan under Moses' guidance around the thirteenth century BC as related in the Bible. It is said that for forty years they wandered in the desert to erase all Egyptian influences and develop their identity.

**guru** a teacher, especially a Brahman in Hinduism who taught the *Vedas* and trained students to become pious Hindus.

**Hamites** African peoples who speak related Hamito-Semitic languages but do not form a cultural or ethnic unit. The Hamites include, among others, the Hausa, Berbers, and Galla.

**Hattusas** (Boghazköy) Hittite city founded in the early seventeenth century BC, which was the capital of the Hittite Empire from 1650 to 1200 BC. The king resided here. The archives found here contain a wealth of information about Hittite society and religion.

**Hattusilis I** Hittite king in the Old Hittite Kingdom from c.1650 to 1620 BC. He founded Hattusas and tried to protect Hittite power against the Hurrians in Syria and the mountain peoples of Asia Minor.

**Hattusilis III** Hittite king in the Hittite Empire from c.1285 to 1265 BC. He made a peace agreement with Egypt around 1269 and was forced to defend his empire against

the Anatolian mountain people, the Sea Peoples, and the rising Assyrians.

**Hebrews** *See* Israelites.

**Hezekiah** king of Judah from c.727 to 698 BC and friend of Isaiah. He introduced reforms to placate Yahweh. He successfully defended Judah against the Assyrians.

**Hittite Empire** period in Hittite history from c.1400 to 1200 BC when the empire reached its greatest expansion into Syria and northern Mesopotamia. Around 1200 the empire suddenly disappeared. Some Syrian and Anatolian cities preserved Hittite culture in separate Neo-Hittite states.

**Hittite king** leader of the Hittites who acted as king, commander of the army, supreme judge, and high priest. His staff consisted mainly of relatives. The queen mother also had a political function and was probably the high priestess.

**Hittite legal code** a hundred or so clay tablets from Boghazköy containing laws and rules having to do with the social organization. It shows that society consisted of aristocrats, serfs, and slaves. There was no wealthy middle class.

**Hittites** peoples from Asia Minor who spoke an Indo-European language and settled in Asia Minor around 2000 BC. They expanded their territory politically southward into Syria, Mesopotamia, and Canaan between 1650 and 1350. The Hittite Empire disappeared around 1200 after the rise of Assyria and invasions by the Sea Peoples.

**Hittite script** from c.2000 on, the Hittites utilized the cuneiform script. Between c.1000 and 700 the Neo-Hittites used hieroglyphs consisting of pictographs and phonetic symbols. Though the cuneiform was deciphered, the hieroglyphs are still not well understood.

**Hittite sun goddess** Arinna, supreme goddess of the Hittites. She was queen of heaven and earth and leader of the kings. The queen mother was probably the high priestess of this national cult.

**Hosea** Hebrew prophet (eighth century BC) who predicted the fall of the Israelites for not obeying Yahweh's commandments and worshiping other gods such as Baal. His prophecies are written in the Old Testament.

**hunters and gatherers** nomadic communities based on the hunting of animals and the gathering of plant foods. They had to survive by unity, equality, and sharing. Due to changes in climate, meat became scarce, and by 8000 BC, the communities in Africa were gradually displaced by agricultural communities.

**Indo-Iranian peoples** nomadic peoples who lived between Mesopotamia and the Indus Valley and may have originated from Central Asia. They included the Persians and the Aryans (Indians) who shared related languages and religions. They separated during the second millennium BC.

**Indra** ancient Indian god of storms, war, and battle. He was portrayed as a warlike hero and is also the rain-giving god of fertility and vegetation. He originates from the prehistoric Indo-Iranian tradition and appears in the *Vedas*.

**Isaiah** Israelite prophet (eighth century BC) who warned against Yahweh's wrath as manifested by the Assyrian threat. This could be averted by unconditional faith in Yahweh and a return to social righteousness. His prophecies are recorded in the Old Testament.

**Israel** Israelite kingdom occupying northern Canaan that split into two after Solomon's death (c.932 BC). The kingdom experienced an economic boom, but was characterized by dynastic instability and moral decay. In 720 Israel was conquered by Assyria.

**Israelites** Semitic tribes who infiltrated Canaan in the second millennium. They probably stayed in Egypt or in the border area between c.1650/1450 and 1214. After 1200 they conquered Canaan, according to the Bible. They lived in a loose alliance of tribes, and from c.1000, joined under a king.

**Jeremiah** Israelite prophet (seventh century BC). He predicted that Judah would fall as a result of the Assyrian threat. He also condemned social injustice as well as the superficial and material honoring of Yahweh. His prophecies are recorded in the Old Testament.

**Jerusalem** capital of the Israelites in Canaan, founded by David around 1000 BC. Originally Jerusalem was a Jebusite city. After Solomon's death, Jerusalem became the capital of the kingdom of Judah. In 586 BC the city was destroyed by the Babylonian king Nebuchadnezzar.

**Judah** a southern region of the Hebrew kingdom that split from the northern kingdom of Israel after Solomon's death (c.925 BC). The kingdom suffered moral decay as the cult of Baal and Astarte expanded. In 586 BC Jerusalem, its capital, was destroyed by the Babylonian king Nebuchadnezzar.

**judge** prior to the united kingdom period, an Israelite leader who assumed military command of the loosely federated tribes in times of emergency. The Bible mentions twelve judges, including Samson.

**Kikuli** Hittite at Hattusas's court who wrote a semiliterary work on the taming and care of horses. The horse trade was an important means of existence for the Hittites.

**Kshatriyas** second hereditary social status in the ancient Indian caste system consisting of princes and noble warriors. They possessed governmental and judicial power and were initially more respected than the Brahmans.

**lineage** (Africa) social group derived from one common ancestor.

**Magellan, Ferdinand** (1480–1521) Portuguese navigator who circumnavigated the globe from 1519 to 1521. He was the first European to reach Oceania and was killed in battle in 1521 in the Philippines.

**magi** mostly Median priests in Iran who adhered to the belief in devas and ahuras that was popular prior to Zoroastrianism. After the death of Zarathushtra, his teachings were modified with the addition of ritual and magical prescriptions.

**Maui** hero in Polynesian creation legend. The Polynesians considered him their patriarch. Under his guidance they left the overpopulated islands of Indonesia and settled in the Polynesian Islands.

**Maurya** major kingdom in India from c.320 to 185 BC. The Maurya dynasty was founded by Chandra Gupta Maurya. The empire reached its zenith and greatest expansion during the reign of Asoka (c.265–236 BC). During this period contact with the Hellenic Greeks increased.

**Medes** nomadic horsemen who settled in Iran during the second millennium. From c.700 they dominated a loose federation of tribes, including the Persians. Together with Babylon, they were responsible for the fall of the Assyrian Empire in 610 BC. In 559 the Persians assumed dominance.

**Melanesia** region in Oceania named by Europeans for the population's dark skin color. It includes, among others, New Guinea, New Caledonia, Vanuatu, the Solomon Islands, and the Fiji Islands. The cultures of the Melanesians vary greatly.

**Melkart-Baal-Tsor** Phoenician god of trade and shipping particularly worshiped in Tyre, where a large temple was dedicated to him; identified with the Greek god Hercules.

**Micronesia** group of islands in Oceania, consisting of small coral islands north of Melanesia, such as the Carolines, Marshall Islands, and Gilbert Islands. The Micronesians display cultural similarities with the Melanesians and Polynesians.

**Moses** Israelite lawgiver and leader who, according to the Bible, led the Exodus from Egypt at Yahweh's command; he probably lived during the thirteenth century BC. He is said to have written the Torah and received the Ten Commandments from God.

**Mursilis I** Hittite king in the Hittite Empire from c.1620 to 1590 BC. He conquered parts of Syria and razed Aleppo and Babylon.

**Mursilis II** Hittite king in the Hittite Empire from c.1350 to 1320 BC. He resided in Hattusas. He defended the empire against the surrounding states, conquered Asia Minor, and fought the Egyptians.

**Muwatallis** Hittite king in the Hittite Empire from c.1320 to 1285 BC. He fought the Egyptians in the battle of Qadesh (1285). The outcome of this battle is unclear, but it was probably a Hittite victory.

**Neo-Hittite Empire** period in Hittite history

from c.1400 to 1200 BC, when the empire reached its greatest expansion into Syria and northern Mesopotamia. Around 1200 the empire suddenly disappeared. Some Syrian and Anatolian cities preserved Hittite culture in separate Neo-Hittite states.

**Oceania** islands in the Pacific Ocean consisting of Australia, Melanesia, Indonesia, Polynesia, Micronesia and New Guinea.

**Old Hittite kingdom** period in Hittite history from c.1700 to 1500 BC in which the kingdom was established in Asia Minor.

**oracle bones** in China large bones that crack and split when heated, from which oracles were divined. During the Shang period the questions and oracular answers were written or engraved in characters on the bones.

**oracle bone script** Chinese script originally used in the late Shang period (c.1250–1050 BC) on oracle bones. It consisted of abstract symbols indicating words or portions of words. From these Shang characters current Chinese ideograms evolved.

**Palestine** (named by the Greeks after Philistine) land along the Mediterranean Sea and to the Arabian desert, inhabited by Semitic tribes (Amorites, Canaanites, Israelites) as well as Hittites and Philistines. Beginning with Israelite kings, much of the area was politically united by c.1000 BC.

**Persepolis** important center of the Persian kingdom of the Achaemenids. From the reign of Darius it also was a major royal citadel with multicolumned halls. Persepolis was destroyed by Alexander the Great.

**Persia** ancient home of several tribes and great civilizations. In c.330 BC the Achaemenid Persian Empire was conquered by Alexander the Great.

**Persians** Indo-Iranian peoples who settled on the Persian plateau during the second millennium BC. They lived as a loose federation of tribes led by the Medes, against whom they rebelled in 558 BC. They then founded a large ancient world empire that was conquered by Alexander the Great around 330.

**Philistines** Indo-European maritime people who settled in coastal Canaan at the end of the thirteenth century BC. They drove out the Israelites and Canaanites from the coastal areas, forcing the Israelite tribes to organize centrally. King David of Israel and Judah ended their expansion.

**Phoenicia** country north of Israel and the Palestinian areas (modern Lebanon) consisting of mountains and a narrow coastal strip. It was inhabited by local groups, mainly Canaanites. After Egyptian rule (c.1500–1350 BC) and Hittite rule (c.1350–1200 BC), Phoenicia became independent around 1000 BC. The Phoenician forests were used for shipbuilding and timber export.

**Phoenician literature** surviving Phoenician texts consist mainly of travel logs, ship journals, and manuals for sailing. They contain

much information about navigation, the sea, and coastal areas. Much of the information was secret because the Phoenicians did not want to reveal their sources of income.

**Phoenician trade settlements** trade settlements founded by the Phoenician cities in strategic locations along the Mediterranean coast, such as Carthage, Marseilles, and Cádiz. They sometimes evolved into cities and had no colonial ties with the mother city.

**Phoenician voyages** Phoenician maritime voyages of discovery and colonization during the first half of the first millennium BC. They explored the West African coast, discovering native tribes and animals, including gorillas.

**Phoenicians** Semitic tribes in coastal Levant since c.1300 BC. They inhabited independent city-states and established trading partners throughout the Mediterranean, in Africa, and the Near East. Around 1000 BC they became the most important navigators in the Mediterranean.

**Polynesia** a group of islands named by Europeans in Oceania east of Melanesia, including Hawaii, Samoa, Tahiti, the Society Islands, New Zealand, and Easter Island. The inhabitants were able navigators.

**Polynesian epics** heroic epics handed down orally that described voyages, discoveries, wars, and revenge. They illustrate Polynesian creation myths, culture heroes, and colonization movements, and the far-advanced Polynesian art of navigation. To these were added supernatural phenomena and lyrical hymns.

**prophets** Israelite wise men who transmitted Yahweh's messages and commandments and predicted the future, as recorded in the Old Testament. They warned against social injustice and worshiping gods other than Yahweh. Only collective piety might avert the people's destruction, they taught.

**Qin** state in western China which existed from 256 to 206 BC. It gradually conquered the Zhou states and politically unified all of northern China in 221. A central government was established, and the feudal system was exchanged for direct government by officials.

*Rig-Veda* earliest sacred document of the Aryans, composed around 1200 BC, which consists of hymns to the gods and incantations of various poets. It mentions thirty-three gods.

**Royal Zhou** central authority during the Zhou dynasty to which all feudal states were initially subject. Gradually the feudal states grew and became more independent, eventually making the king of Zhou a merely symbolic head of these states.

**Sabbath** seventh day of the week and day of rest according to the Ten Commandments of the Israelites. The Sabbath lasts from Friday night to Saturday night. The Sabbath was originally a Mesopotamian institution and was probably given a different religious significance by the Israelites.

**Samson**  one of the judges of the Bible. According to biblical stories, Samson possessed enormous power, the source of which was his long hair. He successfully fought the Philistines until he was betrayed by a Philistine woman, Delilah.

**satrap**  governor of a Persian Empire satrapy. Satraps largely continued the original government and managed the collection of taxes, road maintenance, and security. They were supervised by royal secretaries. Army commanders in satrapies were controlled by the Persian king. When the empire declined, their power increased.

**satrapies**  autonomous provinces governed by the satraps in the ancient Persian Empire that were formed from conquered kingdoms. They largely retained their original government, but paid taxes to the empire and supplied troops in time of war.

**Saul**  Israelite king, c.1025–1000 BC, who was the first to centrally govern the Israelite tribes in Canaan. His rule was not universally recognized. He fought the Philistines and died in battle against them.

**script of Easter Island**  type of script consisting of ideograms found on Easter Island on boards dating from c. AD 1500. It may be a type of stenography with key words representing long tales. It is possibly of non-Polynesian origin.

**Shang culture**  Bronze Age culture in northern China from c.1800 to 1050 BC. The area under the influence of the Shang culture was not politically united, even though a Shang state existed within the territory of the Shang civilization from c.1500 on. The Shang were the first royal historical dynasty. They built cities and produced bronzeware and weapons.

**Shang dynasty**  state governed by Shang kings from c.1600 to 1050 BC. Anyang was the last capital of Shang from the mid-thirteenth to the eleventh centuries BC. Shang kings moved their capitals for reasons not fully understood; the earlier capitals have not yet been archaeologically located. There was a centralized government and cities governed by autonomous vassals in the outlying areas. The populace were generally peasants who leased land from the rulers in the cities and from the king in exchange for labor.

**Shudras**  fourth and lowest rank in the caste system of India, consisting of servants and laborers whose chief duty was to serve the three higher classes. They were considered second-class citizens with few rights, and not allowed to read the *Vedas*. Some groups were avoided by other castes.

**Sidon**  city on the Phoenician coast that was a powerful trading center c.1400–700 BC. Phoenicians were often called Sidonians.

**Solomon**  king of the united kingdom of Israel and Judah from c.965 to 925 BC and son of David. He brought peace and prosperity, promoted trade through foreign relations and infrastructure, and built the Temple of Yahweh in Jerusalem.

**Suppuliumas**  Hittite king of the Hittite Empire from c.1380 to 1335 BC. He expanded the kingdom to its greatest size, conquered Syria with an organized army of charioteers, and fought the Mitanni.

**Susa**  city in southwest Iran that was the winter residence of the Achaemenids in the ancient Persian Empire. Together with Babylon, they formed the administrative and political center of the empire.

**Ten Commandments**  Israelites considered these ethical and religious provisions to be Yahweh's commandments after Yahweh was said to have given them to Moses on Mount Sinai in the desert. They were probably written down at a later time. The first commandment concerned monotheism.

**terra-cotta armies**  thousands of life-sized terra-cotta statues of soldiers and horses found since 1974 near the tomb of the first emperor of Qin (or King Zheng of Qin).

**Teshup**  Hurrian storm god who was adopted by the Hittites and worshiped as the god of storms and war. He was the husband of the Hittite sun goddess Arinna and was considered the king of the heavens.

**Torah**  an aggregate of civil, religious, and ritual laws and rules used by the Israelites. They are ascribed to Moses, but do not reflect nomadic life in the desert; they were probably written down later by priests in Jerusalem.

**Tyre**  Phoenician city situated on an island off the coast of Lebanon. Tyre was a booming trading city in the tenth to seventh centuries BC that founded many colonies, including Carthage. Power was largely in the hands of noble families.

**Ugarit**  northern Canaan (Levant) trading town, a Semitic city-state from the third millennium BC. After reaching its height of power (1550–1360 BC), Ugarit was controlled by the Hittites, but was destroyed around 1200 by the Sea Peoples. Clay tablets from the second millennium BC contain information about Semitic languages and religions. Artifacts prefigure the Phoenician culture to follow.

**Untouchables**  lowest social group in the Indian caste system, which probably originally consisted of indigenous non-Aryan inhabitants. They were placed below and outside the caste system and were considered inferior and, therefore, untouchable. They carried out slave labor and lived on the edge of Aryan settlements.

**Vaisyas**  third inherited social status in the caste system of India, consisting of merchants and farmers.

*Vedas*  earliest Indian literature in the original language of the Aryans, consisting of liturgical texts, ritual formulas, philosophical texts, and legends. They were handed down orally and put into writing much later.

**Vishtaspa**  Persian king c. sixth century BC who was converted to the faith of Zarathushtra. Responsible for spreading the faith, he was probably a local ruler who fought the nomadic Tatar (Tartar) tribes.

**Warring States Period**  last period of the Zhou dynasty through the unification of China, from the early fifth century to 221 BC. War was a constant fact of life, yet trade, agriculture, and urbanization evolved simultaneously. Legislation and philosophy, such as Confucianism, legalism, and Daoism developed.

**water culture**  African culture between 9000 and 2000 BC in northern Africa in the Nile-Sahara territory. Because of the wet climate at that time, many lakes, marshes, and rivers developed. The population subsisted on marine animals and plants and lived in permanent settlements.

**Yahweh**  God of the Israelites, initially a war god who led the movement into Canaan, later a protective god. The Yahweh cult was monotheistic and prohibited other cults, such as that of the fertility god Baal. According to the prophets, Yahweh would punish the people for social injustice and impiety, thus avenging the poor and the oppressed.

**Zarathushtra**  (Zoroaster) founder of the ancient Persian religion Zoroastrianism. A social-religious reformer who lived between the seventh and the sixth centuries BC, his teachings were based on what he saw as the battle between the good Ahura Mazda and the evil Angra Mainyu. By acting, thinking, and speaking properly one supported Ahura Mazda.

*Zend-Avesta*  the holy book of Zarathushtra's religion. It contained stories of creation, liturgical writings, and the history of Persia and its religion. *Avesta* is the part containing the writings, *Zend* is the commentary.

**Zheng of Qin**  king of Qin (221–207 BC) who proclaimed himself Qin Shihuangdi (first emperor of Qin) in 221 BC after all Zhou states had been conquered. He expanded the empire to the north and the south.

**Zhou dynasty**  Chinese culture c.1050–256 BC. Around 1050 the Zhou people, part of the Shang culture from the northwest, overtook the Shang and created many feudal states in northern China. From the sixth century on, their armies relied particularly on infantry and cavalry made up mostly of peasants. The peasants also worked as construction laborers and maintained dikes and irrigation works.

**Zion**  (City of David) one of the two hills on which Jerusalem was built. It was the religious site of the city where the Temple of Yahweh, with the Ark of the Covenant, was located. It was also the source of the sole water supply.

# Bibliography

## The Phoenicians
Baumgarten, A. I. *The Phoenician History of Philo of Byblos: A Commentary.* Leiden, 1981.
Cary, M., and Warmington, E. H. *The Ancient Explorers.* Harmondsworth, 1963.
Harden, D. B. *The Phoenicians.* London, 1962.

## The Influence of the Phoenicians
Craigie, P. C. *Ugarit and the Old Testament.* Grand Rapids, 1983.
Diringer, D. *The Alphabet: A Key to the History of Mankind.* London, 1968.
Hooker, J. T., ed. *Reading the Past: Ancient Writing from Cuneiform to the Alphabet.* London, 1990.
Kloos, C. *Yhws's Combat with the Sea: A Canaanite Tradition in the Religion of Ancient Israel.* Leiden, 1986.
Sass, B. *The Genesis of the Alphabet and Its Development in the Second Millenium BC.* Wiesbaden, 1988.

## The Israelites and Neighboring Peoples
Bright, J. *A History of Israel.* Philadelphia, 1972.
de Geus, C. H. J. *Early Israel: Anthropological and Historical Studies on the Israelite Society before the Monarchy.* Leiden, 1985.
Rappaport, A. S. *Ancient Israel: Myths and Legends.* London, 1987.
Van Seters, J. *Abraham in History and Tradition.* New Haven-London, 1975.
Thomas, D. Winton. *Documents from Old Testament Times.* London, 1958.

## Kings and Prophets
Anderson, G. W. *The History of the Religion of Israel.* Oxford, 1966.
De Vaux, R. *Ancient Israel, Its Life and Institutions.* London, 1973.
Robinson, T. H. *Prophesy and Prophets in Ancient Israel.* London, 1979.
Talmon, S. King. *Cult and Calender in Ancient Israel.* London, 1986.
Yeivin, S. *The Israelite Conquest of Canaan.* London, 1971.

## The Hittites
Gurney, O. R. *The Hittites.* Harmondsworth, 1966.
Macgueen, J. G. *The Hittites and Their Contemporaries in Asia Minor.* London, 1986.
Neufeld, E. *The Hittite Laws.* London, 1951.

## The Early History of China
Barnes, G. L. *China, Korea and Japan: The Rise of Civilization in East Asia.* London, 1993.
Blunden, C., and Elvin, M. *Cultural Atlas of China.* Oxford, 1988.
Fairbank, J. K., and Reischauer, E. O. *China: Tradition and Transformation.* Sydney, 1989.
Gernet, J. *A History of Chinese Civilization.* Cambridge, 1987.
Ramsey, S. R. *The Languages of China.* Princeton, 1989.

## The Persians
Frye, R. N. *The Heritage of Persia.* New York, 1963.
Gerschevitsch, I., ed. *The Cambridge History of Iran: From the Third Millenium BC to the Death of Alexander in 323 BC.* Cambridge, 1983.
Ghirshman, R. *Iran, from the Earliest Times to the Islamic Conquest.* London, 1954.
Nyberg, H. *Die Religionen des alten Iran.* Liepzig, 1938.

## Zarathushtra
Boyce, M. *A History of Zoroastrianism.* 2 vols. London, 1975–1982.
Dandamacv, M. A. *Persien unter den ersten Achameniden (6. Jahrhundert).* Wiesbaden, 1976.
Dawson, M. M. *The Ethical Religion of Zoroaster.* New York, 1969.
Olmstead, A. T. *History of the Persian Empire.* Chicago, 1984.
Schlerath, B., ed. *Zarathrusta.* Darmstadt, 1970.
Zaehner, R. C. *The Teachings of the Magi: A Compendium of Zoroastrian Beliefs.* London, 1975.

## Indo-Europeans in India
Marshall, I. *Mohenjo-Daro and the Indus Civilization.* London, 1931.
Smith, V. *History of India.* Oxford, 1958.

## Cultures of the Pacific
Barclay, G. *A History of the Pacific.* London, 1978.
Burney, J. *Chronological History of Voyages and Discoveries in the South Seas.* New York, 1967.
Layard, L. *Stone Men of Malekula.* New York, 1942.
Mead, M. *Coming of Age in Samoa.* New York, 1929.
Reund, P. *Easter Island.* New York, 1947.
Ward, G., ed. *Man in the Pacific Islands.* London, 1972.

## Africa
Davidson, B. *The Story of Africa.* London, 1984.
De Graft-Johnson, C. *African Glory.* London, 1954.
Gann, L. H., and Duignan, P. *Burden of Empire.* London, 1967.
Murdock, J. P. *Africa.* New York, 1959.
Oliver, R. *The Dawn of African History.* London, 1961.

# Further Reading

Bellerophon Staff. *Ancient China*. Santa Barbara, CA, 1992.

Cotterell, Arthur. *Ancient China*. New York, 1994.

Efron, Benjamin. *Heroes of Jewish History Workbook*. Hoboken, NJ, 1966.

Fox, Mary V. *Iran*. Danbury, CT, 1991.

Garstang, John. *The Hittite Empire*. New York, 1976.

Grainger, John D. *Hellenistic Phoenicia*. Oxford University Press. New York, 1992.

Gurney, O. R. *The Hittites*. New York, 1991.

Jones, Graham. *How They Lived in Bible Times*. Ventura, CA, 1992.

Jones, Constance. *Africa*. New York, 1993.

Knill, Harry. *Ancient Africa*. Santa Barbara, CA, 1993.

Mallory, J. P. *In Search of the Indo-Europeans*. New York, 1991.

Martinet, Andre. *From the Steppes to the Seas: Indo-Europeans*. New Rochelle, NY, 1989.

Moulton, James H. *Early Zoroastrianism*. New York, 1976.

Musgrove, Margaret. *Ashanti to Zulu: African Traditions*. New York, 1992.

Nardo, Don. *The Battle of Marathon*. San Diego, 1995.

Odijk, Pamela. *The Phoenicians*. Morristown, NJ, 1989.

Rajendra, Vijeya. *Iran*. New York, 1990.

Ross, Frank Jr. *Oracles, Bones, Stars, and the Wheelbarrow: Ancient Chinese Science and Technology*. New York, 1990.

Teague, Ken. *Growing Up in Ancient China*. Mahway, NY, 1993.

Wilkins, A. S. *Ancient Phoenicia and Ancient Israel*. Chicago, 1980.

Winn, Shan. *Heroes and Happiness: The Indo-European Roots of Western Ideology*. Lanham, MD, 1995.

# Illustration Credits

# Index

Text is indicated in roman type; illustrations are indicated in italic type.

Text is indicated in roman type; illustrations are indicated in italic type.

Text is indicated in roman type; illustrations are indicated in italic type.

Text is indicated in roman type; illustrations are indicated in italic type.